ABOUT THE AUTHOR

Northern Ireland-based author Sheila P Kelly, began her writing career as a part-time reporter for the Armagh Gazette, reporting on unusual newsworthy stories and social events in her home town Keady, South Armagh on the border with the Republic of Ireland.

In her early 20's as she navigated nursing college and marriage with young kids she had first-hand experience dealing with ordinary people, paramilitaries and security forces who experienced psychological distress during and after the armed conflict. One such person encountered during her nursing duties was a notorious Belfast gang leader who very briefly sought refuge from being arrested while posing as having a nervous breakdown.

She wanted to document the nuances of what happened during the height of the Troubles and began writing this book in the '80s while attending a creative writing course. However, as events unfolded, and the days got busy, constantly running to keep up with her psychiatric work, family, and other responsibilities, time didn't allow for it all to be documented as it happened. Knowing that those stories would eventually fade from memory, she documented some of the stories in more recent years before critical elements were forgotten.

This is a memoir of events she and her husband shielded their young family from during the period of political unrest. A treasured keepsake that they can pass down from generation to generation.

THERE IS NO FLAG WORTH DYING FOR

Sheila P. Kelly

CONTENTS

Irish Street

'Our Che Guevara.'

They would say in low voices in the local dens of iniquity. His elusive behaviour baffled security forces. He was known as 'The Shooter'. Often seen firing his carbine at soldiers along border checkpoints. His terrorist career was featured in The Irish News almost every week. Despite this, he was handsome and was secretly admired by many young women in the area.

Sarah lived on Irish Street. From there, a tributary flowed down into the city's main streets. The City of Armagh, also known as the 'Murder Mile'. In a well-known Nationalist neighbourhood, Sarah's house was one of a row of sensible terraced houses.

Michael, her husband worked in the civil service, forty miles away, so he had to leave early and return late. They had recently welcomed Jude into the world. It was 1971 and Sarah was one of the first nurses to be granted maternity leave. She enjoyed spending time with her baby in their new home.

Jude was irritable and restless one particular morning

as she stepped out their front door with him in his pram to try to settle him. An old-fashioned royal blue pram adorned with a silver metal emblem embossed with the Silver Cross emblem. It was equipped with large springs for easy and smooth movement. She was very proud to own it having paid it off in 6 monthly instalments with Heinz Beans coupons, making it an affordable luxury. As she carefully manoeuvred the wheels over the front step, she knew he would be fast asleep in minutes. Michael reminded her to be careful while out walking.

'Be very careful, don't take risks, it's not worth it.'

She felt happy and carefree that sunny morning, as this rang in her ears. Mick, as he was known by his friends was careful about everything. His timekeeping, car, clothes, and paperwork. Typical civil servant, she mused as she pulled the door closed, carefully placing the key in her shoulder bag while pointing the pram down the street. She saw no soldiers down the slope, at least not as far as the corner. The street turned slightly as it met the cross-roads; this was no cause for concern. All of the doors to the houses were closed as she passed them on the incline. A new thing in their street. The days of leaving your front door open, friendly and welcoming to both friends and strangers were long gone.

Several years before, the UVF opened fire on three Catholic civilians as they left a pub, killing one and wounding the other two. One soldier claimed the shooting was an accident. There hadn't been any more serious incidents in the city since.

Having grown up in a small border town. Sarah was unfamiliar with checkpoints and car searches in the city, believing that these things only took place at the actual border. However, they were mostly left alone on their street on the outskirts of the city. Army jeeps and convoys occasionally passed without incident. Patrols and security were mostly located on the main road into the city.

By avoiding the news, Sarah avoided thinking about her husband's commute to and from work. She coped better with this. Rat-a-tat-tat! Several bullets suddenly pierced through the sky. Leaning against the low wall opposite, a furtive figure held a rifle, she was sure it was a rifle. She had chanced upon an IRA ambush. While instinctively diving down the hill as she grabbed the pram tightly.

'Jesus, Jesus!'

Bullets whistled passed low over her head, as she continued. The little one thankfully remained in his deep slumber. Soldiers swiftly arrived further down the road after hearing the sharp cracking in the air. Their Land Rover came to an abrupt stop in the middle of the road, doors flew open, and a team of soldiers jumped out. Low movements of khaki-coloured uniformed men with rifles pointed at her.

'Ma'am leave the road now!' they yelled at her in strong English accents.

Dear God, Sarah prayed, running as fast as she could while trying to control the pram. Keep us safe.

It seemed like an eternity until Sarah reached the bottom of the street. The Army returned fire on the shooter as an agitated soldier carrying a semi-automatic rifle escorted her across the road. Not knowing where to go, she ran towards a large open arched entryway beside the bookie's shop. Looking back, Sarah witnessed a gunman hopping along the low wall. Taking potshots at the soldiers in sight. It felt like a war zone. She recognized him. Saw him clearly. His wife worked in the hospital with her. Another nurse. They often shared lifts to work.

Feeling vulnerable, afraid, and alone, Sarah checked again on the little one. Thankfully, they were not injured, but she was angry, very angry. As her breath began to even out she detected muffled voices. Around ten people were huddled together further down the dark entryway. She became enraged. It was the only emotion she felt at that time.

'Don't let it get to you love,' whispered an older man standing close. 'Is the wee one all right?' he asked looking into the pram.

Is this normal? Sarah replied while trying to fathom, if they were just so used to this, was this just how they lived? Everything had happened so quickly.

The sporadic gunfire continued. Rat-a-tat-tat! followed by a lull before it started again. As the shots grew louder, a furious fusillade from the soldiers followed. It was impossible to see what was going on from the middle of the arched entryway. After a time, there was a disquieting silence. The nervous group edged to the entrance to peek out cautiously. An explosion of vehicle engines broke the silence and a commanding voice yelled,

'Move out now!'

Once the Army Jeeps had left, the older man emerged first from their refuge. Quickly assuming the role of a watchman, he reported that there was no blood flowing down the hill. Her newfound companions gingerly entered the street. Local businesses gradually started opening their doors again, letting other citizens out. They all fled to their homes. Sarah was last to leave with her high-sprung pram. In times of crisis, it was not designed for quick movement. Running home, she vowed to replace it with one of those fold-up pushchairs that were easier to handle. The alternative route home proved to be longer. All uphill. Overcome with emotion, tears began to flow as she closed the front door and once the panic subsided, she banked the episode in her heart.

Sarah learned that there had been no fatalities through the evening news. No one was killed THIS time. Mick didn't mention the shooting exchange in their street when he returned home that evening. They did not have a phone, and the news had not reached him at work. On the same day, there were more serious incidents across the city. Escalating. No doubt he would hear a version of what happened on their street at some point in the pub. Sarah kept it to herself for now, as well as her desire to flee to her family's hometown on the border.

Their city zone began to experience more incidents. The Army's response was to raid homes at all hours, randomly stop and search people on the streets and set up regular roadblocks. Strangely, very few young men lived on their street, except for Sarah's husband. However, he was no threat. Most of the other homes were occupied by older couples and singles. All descendants of many generations who previously resided there. Neither of the young couple knew anyone living nearby who was involved in any subversive or anti-government groups.

Due to the many nooks and crannies in that ancient city, a gunman could easily enter and exit their street. Little twists and turns from the top of the hill gave way to many escape routes. An older friend informed Sarah about secret gatherings of men in some homes. Hastily organised meetings. Sitting on the stairs and anywhere else bums could rest. Each one with a gun in their hands. 'The Shooter' making an occasional furtive visit.

Several weeks after the shooting incident, Sarah was startled by a heavy knocking at the door followed by a loud English accent. She jumped up and peered out of the curtains. Dear God, something must have happened! She thought. Michael was at football practice and baby Jude was tucked into his cot upstairs for the night. Soldiers with rifles stood guard at her door. Upon reaching the small hallway, she heard a command to, 'Open the door ma'am.' Upon opening, several burly men burst in pointing weapons in all directions.

'We are conducting a search,' she was roughly informed. 'Stand aside.'

Sarah was dumbfounded and shocked as they clumped around the house poking guns under cushions and seats. Opening cupboards and doorways. She did not follow them. She fretted for her baby's safety. They thundered back down the stairs, dispersing as quickly as they arrived, the Soldiers marched to the house next door without explanation nor apology.

The worst was still to come. Raids continued without warning. They became the norm as a result. Advised by other families to confront the intruders going forward, she took a firmer stance every time they came back. In most cases, Mick was at training when they arrived. Sarah continued to demand to know why they were being so heavy-handed. Despite their determined advice for her to stay put, she began following them around the house. The practice of poking a rifle under a sleeping baby's mattress became commonplace. Before they left, she had to make sure no gun was hidden beneath it.

Bomb scares also became commonplace. Forced to leave the house within ten minutes after loud knocks on the door seemed worse than the home searches. The Gas Works building tucked into a recess near the top of the road, was often a target for bomb threats. Evacuations were considered a good excuse to purge houses of strangers hiding out. It became routine in the late evenings to take the sleeping baby out of its cot and run across town with the pram. The all-clear was generally only given well into the night. On those frosty evenings, Sarah's sister-in-law welcomed her. She and her husband lived across the city in a non-Catholic neighbourhood. Their home formally belonged to a much-loved grandfather without religious affiliation. He fought in the second world war.

Sarah and Mick reminisce about those early days often, and Sarah remembers proudly the last bomb scare they experienced on Irish Street. She awoke to the sound of a rifle's butt banging on the door. After working a night shift at the hospital, she was especially tired that evening. Mick was attending a football meeting. Answering the door sleepily she agreed to another order to leave the house for the night. Hearing the commotion at the neighbouring homes, she wearily dragged herself back upstairs after locking the door. Gently lifting her sleeping baby she took him into the back spare room and snuggled down with him thinking if The Gas Works do blow up, at least we are at the back of the house and comfortable in bed. Until the next day, that was all she remembered.

Waking up to loud shouting, Sarah answered the door once again. It was Michael pale and trembling.

'What happened to you? Everyone else has been down below the cordoned-off area. I stood there in a panic all night. I even went to my brother's home. Mary said you hadn't arrived'.

When she settled him down, she could not explain anything

other than the need for sleep.

As they muddled through those troubled times, he offered long-winded advice for future times like those.

The house they lived in had been gutted and renovated before they had purchased it. With the option to receive substantial compensation through a vesting order, the local authority encouraged the reluctant couple to move. The offer was accepted with mixed feelings. After becoming accustomed to 'the going's on', content in their first home, the court order gave them no choice but to move. Despite that, a new development of houses came on the market on the outskirts of the city with easy access to the countryside. The young couple bought a semi-detached house there and looked forward to a new beginning. Away from their early exposure to the unrest in the other part of the city. The gossip about 'The Shooter' faded into the background.

'Our Pub' Lights Out

N ot always in prayer. My nerves jangled as I drove up
the road behind the police cars, ambulances, and
fire trucks in my noisy old yellow VW Beetle. Please God
let them all be safe.

'You need to come home. Now Sarah,' my cousin had
shouted down the phone. 'Something awful has happened.'
After kissing my husband goodbye and giving him a few
garbled instructions regarding the children, I headed for
my hometown to check up on my parents. Knowing they
were okay did not calm my fear or sense of shock.

Rosie called me that autumn evening to tell me that
a bomb had exploded in 'Our Pub'. She explained that
my mom and dad needed assistance. Their home and
bicycle shop on the other side of the street had taken some
of the blast. Thankfully they were not injured, but they
were clearly shaken, and the building was badly damaged.
Fortunately, they were both in the kitchen behind the
shop when it went off.

'Jesus, Mary, and St. Joseph!' I repeated to myself.
I arrived in the centre of town in ruins. Through the fading

smoke, I could see bricks, wood, glass shards and clothing scattered everywhere among small fires that had not been distinguished yet. Roofs had been stripped of slates, chimneys were twisted, and brickwork was askew. That sight remains ingrained in my mind. Parking near Rosie's home, located on a slight slope, I could see that the area was not yet cordoned off. It was dark and eerily silent with no one around and the streetlights were out. Only the flashes of the emergency crew headlights could be seen as they leapt out of the trucks at the bomb site. Their sirens were now silent.

Our Pub was the heart and soul of our wee border town. This was 1976, and the Northern Ireland conflict had not yet affected people too much in our border town. It was referred to as 'Our Pub' by most people due to its open house policy. All denominations were welcome, but only a few Protestants attended. Family-oriented, it was a hub of social life in the town. Aside from club meetings, birthday parties, anniversaries, fundraising events, and pub quizzes, many traditional Irish music sessions were held there.

The pub was owned by a young couple in their 30s. Tom ran a tidy no-nonsense bar. He regularly turfed out rowdy customers and refused to serve drunk and underage customers. He was highly respected in the town. Eilish, his wife, helped run the events and often relieved him on quiet evenings in the early part of the week. She also helped in winter when Tom unofficially extended the opening hours for the locals. The local RUC turned a blind eye to this. The young couple lived just down the road from my parents' shop and home. Across the street from their pub.

A policeman was kind enough to allow me access to my parent's house before the area was cordoned off. Torch in hand, I stepped over the street rubble to enter the shop through the broken front door. Stepping gingerly over broken glass, mangled bicycles and a host of smaller debris scattered across the floor. My heart pounded as I reached the kitchen behind the store.

Rosie was busying herself making tea while consoling my parents. It was a few hours after the bomb attack, and they were seated looking relaxed and at ease. The kitchen seemed to be relatively intact. Only a few broken windowpanes were visible. All bedrooms and bathrooms were located at the front of the building, so I knew the upstairs would be in ruins.

Amidst tears and relief, my nursing habits quickly kicked into gear. As I asked my parents if they were hurt and how they were feeling, I took their pulse. Father hugged me and mother nodded, unable to rise from her chair. I suspected she had taken a little Valium that she kept for stressful situations. Many were not without their periods of depression during the war and Valium was prescribed quite freely back then to women of a certain age. Tears swelled in her eyes.

The story of the bomb unfolded. No warning was given. The pub was hosting a birthday celebration that was due to start at 8 pm around the time it exploded. Several people were wounded, some with life-threatening injuries. There may have been a few deaths. According to rumours, a local lad was seriously injured.

That evening, Rosie and I climbed upstairs to find shattered bulbs and lights everywhere. We shone torches around the rooms to see the extent of the damage. Through shards of glass and with the help of the emergency lighting that had been switched on outside we could see the full impact of the blast. We knew there must have been some deaths. Not everyone would have survived.

Broken tiny slivers of glass clung to every surface. Furniture, curtains, carpets, beds, and mattresses. Rosie filled me in on that destructive evening while we worked long and hard to make one bedroom habitable. How the survivors and their families were persuaded to go home in case a secondary device was detonated. Only the immediate family of the injured remained, in a cordoned-off area directly in front of Our Pub. To await the arrival of emergency services along with some local off-duty nurses and a doctor.

Observing the news reporters and TV cameras arriving from the shattered upstairs window, Rosie elaborated on what had happened.

'Jesus Sarah, that was young Larry Lenneghan's party. It was his 18th birthday. The Party was set to start at 8 pm and everyone was getting ready to arrive on time. When they left their homes, it was very dark. The town lights were out. Switched off possibly.'

Rosie was generally very accurate and swore the lights normally turned on at 7 pm during late Autumn. Rosie was invited to the party, but she planned to go a little later since she lived relatively close. Peeking out the front door, up the hill towards the pub, she noticed the darkness. Both the music and the revellers were chattering loudly.

'Only a few cars parked nearby,' she said quietly. 'Good 'auld pioneers like me.' Pioneers were members of the Catholic Faith who wore pins to let others know they were teetotalers. They voluntarily signed up for their exclusive club and were usually good and righteous people. Always joining in the pub joviality.

I couldn't spend the night with my parents as our youngest daughter was just a baby. Noticing her absence, I tried alerting my other sister by phone, to ask her to watch out for them as she lived just a short walking distance away. I wondered if her husband was out. As a member of the Ministry of Agriculture, he was sometimes required to visit farms late in the evening to advise on emergency problems. Or was her absence due to some cautious fear of a second explosion? Was she just held back by the Police because of the cordoned-off area? Rosie was also unable to contact her when she tried earlier. She usually kept an eye on our parents, continually checking in to see how they were doing, so I let those thoughts slide.

I glanced at my watch and realised it was 3 am. Rosie had long since left. My mother had gone to bed having been persuaded to take one of her Valium tablets to help relax her. Smoking was her former relaxation method. The pills replaced that. My father sat closer to the stove smoking his pipe, deep in thinking. His forehead was wrinkled heavily with worry.

Although we often debated the paramilitaries' actions, I did not discuss the injustice of this bomb with my father. We often argued about his brother, my uncle, who fought for the Republic of Ireland during the '20s. As a nurse, I agreed with my mother who often interrupted our discussions with her viewpoint that all life is precious by saying, 'there is no flag worth dying for.'

After undoing the bolting mechanism which was surprisingly intact, I wearily stepped out over the glass and debris in the bicycle shop once again, forcing open one side of the heavy, damaged door. An old, two-sided door with many layers of paint, a throwback to its former life when our shop was a pub. I noted the full extent of the mess. The old glass-plated window was entirely shattered but roughly boarded up by our wonderful neighbours, and the beautiful old etched Dunlop tyre sign was in pieces. Luckily, the walls of our home were made of old, thick stone, which prevented them from being destroyed. We lived across from the pub that was bombed, but 'Our Pub' was partially hidden on a street corner on a road out of town, so the full impact of the blast was deflected away from us. As I closed the door, two stretchers were loaded into the ambulance. The sight of the covers pulled over bodies on the stretchers caused me to break down in tears.

The street was cleared very quickly, and the footpath was sealed off. As I watched this unfold, I lost track of time in my sadness. How I managed to reach my car and get safely home to my husband that night is a mystery to me. I collapsed into his arms as he helped me to bed. Tears flowed as he hushed me off to sleep.

The following day, both TV and radio broadcast the full story. As the days slowly passed, our sense of time blurred and we, my family and the people of the town picked up our lives once more. The friendly people of the town were broken-hearted and bereaved. Their sorrow was palatable every time anyone was interviewed by the media. But life went on and I returned to my nursing duties as soon as my maternity leave was over, putting the fact that my husband worked in the more troubled Belfast out of my mind. I just needed sleep which was essential after two days of night duty. Thankfully the eldest child was at school, and the youngest was picked up by the baby minder so that I could rest.

A week later, after my ward's patients were settled down for the night, the nurses and I watched the late news. The funerals of the two who died in that bomb brought tears to my eyes once again. The pain was too great for me to stop them from freely flowing and I needed to be comforted for quite some time.

The blast took the life of my neighbour and good friend Michael. His family was devastated, and the town's residents were still overwhelmed by profound sadness and shock. He was three years younger than me. We became friends during our roller-skating sessions every Thursday in the local parish hall. I was quite good at skating and enjoyed dancing, so we also went to other clubs for roller dancing. Michael used to accompany us. His parents knew I would watch out for him. Our friendship blossomed as we roller-skated all over the county and in 1970, he attended my wedding with his then-girlfriend. The other casualty was a mother of three. Her husband, a well-known and respected person in town, never recovered from her death.

When I think back on that day, I can't help recalling Rosie's comments about the streetlights going out the evening of the party in 'Our Pub'. Rosie had thankfully delayed her departure to the party for some reason. Back then, the police had access to electricity controls in some border towns. The electricity station was located within the newly constructed high walls of the Lisdonowen police station at the time. Did the lights go out by coincidence or was there another reason? We may never know. However, an investigation into the incident focused on a murderous gang that lived on a farm back then. As my mother used to say, 'the truth will come out.'

Polly

'I will never forgive those bastards for what they did to my beloved Brendan and our children.' She screamed at me, shaking with venom. There is no forgiveness in my heart. They believe they are on 'our side.' There are no sides, only murderers. I will never be able to forgive them. I can't imagine how I and our children will cope without him. He was our rock.' I just hugged her tighter unable to offer my friend soothing false words.

While pulling the Medicine Trolley out of the ward, I was startled by a voice behind me.

'Hello nurse,' she said.' My name is Polly McGlone. 'Sorry, I'm a little late, I had trouble parking. It is my first day as an assistant nurse on your ward.' This was the first time that I remember meeting Polly.

Polly's voice was gentle, and quiet. She was older than I, perhaps in her late 30s and looked eager and pleased to see me. I couldn't place her even though she knew who I was.

I introduced Polly to the other nurses and the tasks she was expected to accomplish. After several hours of duty, we quickly got acquainted during our breaks.

Observing her pleasant and kind manner with the patients, I knew we would get along well. In no time, we began travelling together for work. We lived close together, so it was convenient, and we became great friends. At first, it seemed like heaven, and it was. Polly's older children provided us with an endless supply of babysitters.

Polly and Brendan lived at the edge of the large Greenfields council estate with a Gaelic Field below it. There were two entrances to the estate. The second entrance was beside us, near Polly's home but their home was not visible from our doorstep.

The homes in the estate were occasionally raided by the Army and the UDR, accompanied by the Police (RUC), where they claimed that known subversive fractions lived and met. These illegal meetings usually took place in the late evenings when we were comfortable at home, so we weren't always aware of them.

One evening a badminton friend whispered to me that she had to leave early so that she could attend one such meeting. She also lived in Greenfields. Elaborating on the meetings in a neighbour's home, she explained how well they were attended. Every man, woman, and child sat in every corner of the house, and every man on the stairs held a gun in his hand. During a dawn raid in our City of Armagh on, the 9th of August 1971, many young men were forced from their beds in Greenfields and interned. Jailed without trial. They weren't the first group to have been interned during this period. Up until then, life was relatively peaceful where we lived and as the years passed, our other children began to arrive. Marie, our third child was wonderful when born. She did not suffer from colic like her elder brother and sister. She fed easily and slept well, smiling up at us each morning. Two years later another sister, a restless little one who needed more attention arrived. Having completed our dream little family, I left my permanent nursing position for a few years to be a full-time mom, relieving their granny of much of her babysitting help.

During the vicious winter of 1980, a bomb was detonated one evening without warning. We were enjoying quiet family time at home watching our newly acquired black and white television. The sudden loud boom shocked us. We quickly grabbed the kids and lay on the floor, reacting instinctively. We had a lot of practice. The entire house shook. Having heard our front living room window smash as it blew out, we watched in nervous shock as the kitchen ceiling above our heads cracked from end to end. The back door of the kitchen flew open. I whispered pleading prayers as we comforted our children and tried to remain silent and still. After the blast, it was silent for what seemed like a long time, so we cautiously got up and huddled together. As we gingerly peered out the back window, we saw smoke billowing in clouds toward the sky. A family friend and neighbour Seamus that lived behind us where a sheer drop led down to his house waved frantically from his garden, asking us to remain in our home.

He could see where the bomb went off.

After what seemed like an eternity, fire sirens and armoured vehicles roaring in the distance broke the silence. Events from our early married life followed us to our new sanctuary. Then the phone rang. Brendan, Polly's husband, assured us his family were safe and that the local shop close to them, had been bombed. Luckily it was closed that late evening. Nobody was injured. The Army ordered them to leave so they went to stay with relatives. Polly's home was closer to the blast and suffered more damage than ours.

Several months after we received compensation for the damage to our home, we began to forget. We forgot about the bomb explosion, believing it was the end of our concerns and worries. Sadly, that wish did not come to pass.

1980, two days after Christmas, Brendan a hard-working labourer who built new homes with his brother was murdered. He was a fit man who enjoyed exercising on weekends. In his early twenties, he joined the Territorial Army (TA) part-time, helping to fulfil his exercise needs. Consequently, he became a target or what so-called terrorists called a 'legitimate target' on account of joining. The new buzzword as reported by the media.

I will never forget going to Polly's home when I finally mustered up the courage to visit. It was unusually quiet. The children were elsewhere, perhaps with relatives.

'Sarah!' She cried louder than usual.

Polly had a lovely soft, cultured, way of speaking. I had always imagined she came from a big wealthy country home. In an unassuming way, she was well-educated and clever. Truly a lady of gentle nature. It was a shock to hear 'I will never forgive those bastards' come out of her mouth. Still, in shock, she informed me of what happened while moving items around in her kitchen chest freezer. He was being watched. Noting his behaviour patterns, the time and the route he took home. They awaited his arrival. He was unceremoniously shot while travelling home in broad daylight from work as he approached his front door. Looking up from the freezer after she calmly explained that she may need extra food for people coming to her home. The area of the shooting was cordoned off below our homes. Visitors other than close family members were not allowed to visit yet. I was the first. We hugged each other, lost for words, and wept a lot. There were no comforting words I could offer her.

The two of us alone in her kitchen was surreal. It was eerily silent outside. The hearse was due to arrive that evening with her husband's remains, but I knew it would soon become a busy hub of people and reporters once his remains had been brought home. I made my way home late that evening feeling a little more comfortable in the knowledge that her relatives had arrived. They were now in charge of making tea and greeting the crowds of people who came to the wake.

The Irish wake is a celebration of life, one last gathering

or party to honour the deceased. The name 'wake' comes from unknown diseases that plagued the Irish countryside and caused some to appear dead. As the family began to mourn, they would awaken. For this reason, the body is waked in the deceased's home for at least one night. 'Irish Wakes' for those who died of unnatural causes were now so frequent in our city. As a result, Armagh became known as 'The Murder Mile', after the many bombs, shootings, and murders on both sides bound for a common destiny of war. Protestants and Catholic police, the Army, or anyone deemed to have played a role in the civil war were targeted. Thinking over it all made me shudder. Eager to return to my own home. Glad that our wee family was intact. When he unbolted the door, I gave my husband the longest hug I could muster while sobbing.

We all moved away from that part of the city as our families grew up. Even today when I bump into Polly by accident, we look into each other's eyes and remember those most awful of times. Slowly, we ask how things, and each other's families are. It is still too painful to discuss what happened. We both acknowledge that there is no forgiveness for all that murder and mayhem that so profoundly affected us and will affect us forever.

Laughing

Stifling a laugh, Sarah knew what was about to happen as the fast-approaching Land Rover arrived in the middle of Thomas Street. She couldn't help but laugh out loud as two Soldiers jumped from the war machine, rifles in hand. Sarah's husband was always so careful. He measured everything he did, but this time he was out of his comfort zone. He had a laid-back attitude on weekends, especially. Deep down Sarah knew he would cope. Hoped he would cope. The entire episode felt surreal. It lasted for a few minutes only.

'It all happened so fast. I didn't give them time to speak. When I pulled out my civil service ID, they knew I was not just anyone. They were dumbfounded when I told them whom I knew, naming a top Northern Ireland Civil Servant while writing down their badge numbers in my pocket notebook. So, they let me out quickly without saying a word.'

Kate, her cousin, and Jim arrived the night before. A Friday. Shara, their large Alsatian dog, lay sprawled out on the back seat of their sporty metallic blue Triumph Herald as they had travelled from Gorey, County Wexford in Southern Ireland. They chose to take the narrow, winding country roads so that they could stop frequently to exercise the dog along the way. The couple arrived tired.

Mick and Jude prepared the usual full Irish breakfast on Saturday morning. Together with the children's enthusiastic chatter, the morning was a resounding success. Mick's walking, sightseeing tour of Armagh City Cathedrals was highly anticipated by the four adults. After breakfast, they set off for the day.

Shara, the dog, stayed behind in the care of Jude, the eldest son. Mick feared she might react badly to the Soldiers if they were present in the city. She was always on guard, protecting her owners, barking fiercely when strangers approached.

As they entered the city centre Sarah's cousins were amazed at the number of troops with rifles filtering through the busy Saturday crowd. The town was buzzing with gatherings of young people catching up in small groups. Mobile phones had not yet infiltrated the population at that time, as they were too expensive for teenagers to purchase. Occasionally, Soldiers stopped to talk with the teenagers in a more intimidating than friendly way. Sarah stopped to greet her neighbour's son and loitered briefly as a Soldier was questioning him a little too insistent. She remained until he moved away.

Kate was a little quiet. She was moved by how relaxed people were, walking about in the presence of the armed

Soldiers on foot patrol. Suddenly, two police Jeeps sped into the city centre street and screeched to a stop. Young policemen poured out of the back doors. An all-Protestant police reserve in black leather jackets, black berets, and black trousers with rifles. Moving swiftly, they infiltrated the streets. Detested by Catholics, the invading troops were dubbed 'The Belfast Black Jackets' by the people of Armagh. They were sent to various towns and cities as part of their training. Sarah's cousins were becoming increasingly nervous, the complacency, lack of irritation, and generally relaxed attitude of everyone baffled them. The bombing of the city buildings had not yet happened, it did however happen a few years later in 1987.

Mick deftly steered the little party, out of the main area, into a quieter part of town, Thomas Street. He knew they could easily access the little lanes leading up the hill from there to visit the two famous cathedrals, eventually returning home via the outer minor road. Admiring the boutique shops in the narrow street along the way, the foursome began to relax again, looking forward to lunch at the Palace Stables highly rated restaurant. Another historic area of Armagh.

Halfway down the street, Sarah glanced in the butcher's window and was surprised to see friction in the opening of the butcher's shop. Inching closer to the shop, she was irritated to see two Soldiers intimidating a young teenager. He was pinned tightly in the doorway with a rifle placed flat across his chest. He looked terrified.

'Are you okay? She asked over the Soldiers' shoulders in a firm voice.

Having moved closer to Sarah, Mick whispered, 'Come on Sarah, this is none of our business.'

Kate and Jim stood in nervous silence behind him. The young man was shaking. He was about seventeen, Sarah knew, he needed her help.

'Move away now mam', the Soldier with the rifle pressed against the boy's chest replied crossly.

The second Soldier turned around and lowered his gun but did not speak. Sarah felt Mick move even closer to her.

'What is the problem with this young man? Can't you see he is frightened?' Mick asked purposefully.

'I'm shopping and am looking for a nice cut of meat for dinner,' Sarah quickly added, 'I would like to enter this shop.'

Watching the terrified youth, she resolved not to move. Out of the corner of her eye, Sarah noticed the second Soldier talking quietly into the walkie-talkie clipped to his collar. Mick moved closer to the young man, asking if he needed to be accompanied home, adding that he would not move until the young lad had been left alone. Suddenly, the situation relaxed, and the Soldiers stepped aside and walked away calmly. The lad, seemingly recovered, stated he was okay and wanted to walk home on his own. While he looked mostly calm, he was still shaking a little as he hurried off muttering his nervous thanks.

An Army jeep suddenly arrived in the narrow street,

halting abruptly, beyond them. Several Soldiers leapt out of the back door and walked swiftly in their direction. Mick, who was engrossed in explaining the incident to their friends was unaware of their approach.

Sarah giggled as she imagined what would follow. And it did. Mick was lifted off his feet, taken swiftly down the street and unceremoniously chucked into the back of the Jeep with the engine still running. Her cousins were speechless. They appeared to shrink beside her. It all happened so quickly. Knowing the worst that might happen, Sarah was not concerned. The worst outcome would be if Mick was sent to the local police barracks. His job worked in his favour. She couldn't help laughing and tried to stifle her reaction. Mick always carried his civil service picture ID with him, they lived in a neutral trouble-free part of town and the name Keeley had no one-sided connotations. She was not worried. Suddenly, the Jeep doors opened again, and Mick jumped out. The vehicle moved away as quickly as it had arrived, roaring up the road, closing its doors in the process.

Noting their visitor's shock over the events that had just unfolded, they suggested leaving Thomas Street to being their tour and climbed the short lane to Saint Patrick's Cathedral Church of Ireland. As they admired the distant city below, Sarah's visitors seemed relieved. On the conveniently placed tourist bench, they discussed the morning's episodes and 'The Black Jackets' patrol. And queried did they confine their known intimidating personal searches, to the city centre? Or did they go somewhere else?

Kate and Jim had never fully realised the daily mayhem that went on in the Keeley lives. Their only knowledge of the bombings, shootings, and deaths came from the news. People in Wexford and throughout the Republic of Ireland largely ignored the events in the north. Mick explained the ins and outs of how things worked for them. The house-to-house searches, roadblocks, car searches and barricades in certain areas of towns. How young men were continually stopped and harassed, women's handbags were searched and how one could attract more searching depending on where one lived. He tried to explain the religious affiliations that divided people and how people reacted to large civil disruptions. Protestant roadblocks and standoffs hemmed in hospital staff preventing them from travelling home. People's reactions to police shootings, murders of members of all sections of society, bombings, and the support for various causes from different communities that were devoted to long-held beliefs. Mick described how the Catholic community boycotted Protestant businesses, bringing their businesses to their knees. In addition, he mentioned the sudden helicopter activity and sirens warning of a pending bomb, and the sound of gun battles regularly crackling in the distance. Sarah, rescuing her cousins from Mick's tirade, spotted a nice new cafe up the hill and suggested they stop for some refreshments. While enjoying the view and peace, her cousins found it incomprehensible that any normal life could go on in all the chaos.

When the visitors returned home, Shara's welcoming barks and excitement prompted them to take her for a walk. Delighted to be invited, the older Keeley children also joined, excitedly setting off for a stroll across the nearby fields. As Mick helped Sarah to clear away the dishes from the morning's fry, he told her what happened in the back of the Army jeep. Sarah knew that he had embellished his experience.

A sudden and loud explosion, while they were finishing up, took them by surprise as their large kitchen window shook. Beyond the fir trees that hugged their garden and low buildings beyond that, fresh, angry, columns of smoke rose upwards in the sky. On seeing a ragged shape float briefly in the air before dropping, Sarah shouted, 'Oh my god.'

This was not like the debris of bricks or vehicle parts.

'Oh my god,' she repeated. 'That was a body.'

It all happened so quickly. There was no warning of a pending bomb. Mick, hugging her tightly wasn't so sure. To calm her down, he reminded her that the children had left for their walk some time ago. By now, they would be well across the fields with their cousins. They have set off on their ramble in the opposite direction, he explained. The younger children were also safe across town playing at their aunt Lizzy's home.

Taking a short walk to find out what had happened was something they wanted to avoid, so Sarah and Mick settled themselves with a cup of tea. While smoking, Sarah nervously told Mick that she was certain she had seen a body floating in the air.

When the dog walkers returned, they played down the incident, waiting to learn if the group had heard the bang. It wasn't the loudest bomb. It was sharp and sudden but duller than the bombings of buildings in cities. As they boiled the kettle for more tea Kate and Jim remarked on hearing a distant bang and wondered about the police presence near the house on their return. Mick downplayed what may have happened, so they accepted there had been an incident or even a crash while Sarah made excuses for her wet face, saying the onions she was chopping for dinner were causing her eyes to water.

They ensured that their guests enjoyed their evening with light-hearted conversation and purposely didn't turn on the TV. Louise danced her favourite Irish dances for them and her younger siblings, having returned from Aunt Lizzy's, went outside to play with the dog. Jude though was very quiet. He didn't join in the 'craic'. Sarah assumed he was thinking of his return to Magee University in Derry the following evening Sunday.

The weekend ended well. The visitors planned their return to Wexford starting early the next morning and then everyone settled down to watch a VHS movie. Mick and Sarah kept the TV off on Sunday as well, knowing the bomb would fill the Sunday news with horror. They knew that someone had died. Someone they may know.

Another life lost.

Jude

With the little ones in bed, the Keeley home began to settle down. Kate and Jim were well on their way back to Wexford. Mick was opening a bottle of Merlot in the kitchen. Still reeling from the shock of the explosion, he needed to relax with a glass of his favourite red.

The evening TV news reported that Mick's former neighbour, a twin, had been killed in a car bombing. They had witnessed the explosion from their kitchen window earlier that day. He was wrongly believed to be in the UDR. His father-in-law was killed by the Provisional IRA near the same spot in 1976. It brought back recent memories of their 38-year-old friend. His wife and children were still in mourning. A few years earlier, he was a sergeant in the TA. They were no longer safe where they lived in Armagh.

Sarah was also containing her shock. Is it any wonder that Armagh is referred to as The Murder Mile? Within just a few hundred yards of their home, in a quiet mixed-religion neighbourhood, there had now been three murders of neighbours and friends. Hearing the pop of the cork she glanced at Jude, who was sitting quietly in a brooding mood.

'What's wrong?' Sarah probed.

'I need to speak with you,' Jude answered. 'I have to ask you something before my lift arrives.'

Jude was offered a degree course in Information Technology at Magee University after passing his A levels. He was the eldest child of six. Sarah and Mick were thrilled. Northern Ireland's politics in the eighties ensured that every community had access to university education. Financial grants enabled students to pursue their dreams.

Quiet by nature. The 'craic' or the conversation didn't start with Jude, but he joined in easily with friends and family. Leaving home to live and study in Derry was going to be a little daunting for him. Despite his laid-back ways, his mother knew he would settle in without much difficulty. He would soon make long-lasting friends.

Throughout Northern Ireland, bombs and shootings continued. Derry City was a particularly troubled city in the mid-1980s, with near-daily rioting similar to other major cities. Derry had the same advantages as studying in Belfast since the Magee campus belonged to the University of Ulster.

Despite the bloody chaos in Ireland, the Keeley parents managed to subdue their worries about their children's whereabouts during this time. On the morning of his enrolment, they travelled from Armagh to Magee to drop off their son. He was not in good form. The night before his departure, he celebrated with his friends at the local pub where he worked as a bartender, to earn money to sustain him while studying for his degree. The farewell lasted until the wee hours of the morning. As he trudged up the avenue, he moaned,

'Why did I agree to come to this godforsaken place?' Knowing her son's usual mood after a night of drinking, Sarah ignored his comment. Seeing the University in a quiet area of the city gave her peace of mind. A calm oasis away from the mayhem of the inner city.

While Mick poured wine and arranged crisps and goodies in the sitting room, Jude began talking about university. He was now in the second year of his studies and was adjusting well. He enjoyed Derry and had made great friends. One of his travelling companions was from Armagh as well.

Sarah was nervous about the conversation with Jude, wondering if he wanted to leave University or if he just needed a loan. She was taken aback by his seriousness so close to his return. He nodded toward the front room as he moved towards it. He had something to tell her alone. She wondered why this secrecy was necessary.

'I have been approached and asked to join. What do you think?' he blurted out with his eyes fixed on hers. 'I have been thinking I should. Others in my year have already joined. What do you think? I need your advice.'

Sarah was stunned. Above all, she did not expect that this would be asked or even considered. She searched for an appropriate response.

Jude had heard his grandfather's stories of the old IRA and his great uncle's role in the Irish Rebellion. These stories, especially his great uncle's activities during the 1920s when the war for independence resurged, sounded exciting and glamorous. The story of how he survived, later joined the new Irish Army after a large section of Ireland became a republic, and how his family continues to receive his Irish Republican pension to this day.

Understanding the lure of a young man living in the largely nationalist Derry, it was clear to Sarah why Jude wanted her advice. He wanted to help in their war. To do the right thing and follow others who were joining the newly formed IRA splinter group. The INLA.

'Jude please listen. You are asking for my advice. I advise you to not join that group. As nurses, we see a lot of young men who are maimed or have died for the cause. We uphold all treatments that will preserve, cure, nurse, and keep ill people alive as part of our nursing responsibilities.' Sarah struggled to find the right words to convince him. 'Please understand you should not do this. I will always remember your grandmother firmly telling my brother, your uncle when he had hinted at helping the cause, that 'there is no flag worth dying for.'

After some lengthy discussion, Jude seemed convinced. Hugging Sarah, he said.

'I just needed you to say that Ma. I felt confused. Now I know what to do'.

Mick was not informed of their conversation at the

time. Sarah knew he had enough on his plate. He was reeling from the death of someone he grew up with and was worried about his travels to and from Belfast for work.

Jude did not join. Sarah knew he didn't as he continued to return home each weekend seemingly happy to work in the pub, serve behind the bar, and enjoy the company of his friends and cousins.

In her advancing years, Sarah finds herself reminiscing about those horrific times. As if in a dream. A dream so real that she would be confused when woke up and relieved to know it was just a dream. She wonders how her family survived in such a bitter and divided place. They were lucky to survive and remain safe in 'The Murder Mile'.

Disappeared

'Shocking,' was the word used by the people in our town. Everyone was discussing the atrocity.

Children who stay out after dark could disappear. They would be taken away by the fairies. There are more fairies in the Grove than anywhere else, according to my mother.

Our favourite place to play in the 1950s was a small half-field near the railway line behind our homes. We loved sliding down it on thick cardboard in the snow. Summer was spent knee-deep in wildflowers and grasses, picking wildflowers, drinking Sun Cap juice, and eating jam-filled sandwiches in the Grove.

We lived near the edge of Lisdonowen, a small old mill town. Our house was one of a row on the edge of town that sloped down the hill at the back of the family bicycle shop. Outhouses and gardens were located behind the basements of houses in generous backyards. Separated from fields and a railway by a narrow stream.

The kitchen window, located above the basement, allowed our mother to keep an eye on us. It was easy for her to call us home from behind the hen loft at the bottom of the garden. Both my cousin Patrick and I loved the Grove. We would skip home when the light dimmed out of hunger and fear of the fairies, so calling us was rarely necessary.

It was widely discussed what had happened. The taxi driver who was shot on the bridge outside of town had a routine. On Wednesdays, he picked up an elderly gentleman at the same time and drove him to Armagh to visit his sister. He served part-time as a UDR soldier, a recently formed government organization. Similar to the Black and Tans of old. Both Protestants and Catholics were invited to join. Locals whispered to each other that this man was a legitimate target. Although they never claimed responsibility, the 'Official IRA' was known to have carried out the attack. The 'Troubles' had come home. News of Belfast and Derry was no longer a dominant focus of headlines. Aside from the burning of homes and businesses most of them owned by Catholics, attacking and threatening residents and bomb scares, there were also sporadic shootings at the police and UDR. County Armagh also had its own 'Troubles'. What a soft name for those bloody times.

After coming out of the bad bend through the bridge and the dip in the road, my 'clapped out' Triumph Herald struggled up the hill. Passing the demarcated place where the awful murder happened.

'There is no flag worth dying for,' my mother used to say. I found the killing to be pointless. The needless loss of life. He was someone's husband, father, brother, or son.

All of life was dear to me as a nurse, from cradle to grave. Healing broken bones, minds, and hearts is one of its main objectives. I was sure someone's heart would never mend because of it.

British soldiers were deployed to Northern Ireland in 1969. Paddy and I had a lot to discuss when they arrived the week before my leave. I dropped by my cousin's house down the street that August evening, but he wasn't there. His sisters were restless, picking at things, such as their nails and lips and objects around them. Vague about his whereabouts. They seemed to be hiding something.

Patrick was the second youngest of the Murphy family. Everyone called him Paddy. He was a year younger than me. We remained best friends during our teenage years. My nursing training took me away from Lisdonowen, near the border of South Armagh, but we kept in touch. As a keen biker, Paddy often crossed the border with his friends to Monaghan or Castleblayney. He would always inform his family before embarking on a journey.

'Did he mention where he was going and how long for?' I asked.

Peter, the youngest of the house chirped in with, 'Paddy hasn't slept in his bed since last night, so he's missing. It looks like he's gone.'

'Don't talk nonsense,' my grumpy uncle John interrupted and cut him off. 'Don't listen to that little whippersnapper, he muddles everything up. I'm sure Paddy will be home soon.' He said.

The conversation quickly shifted. The girls inquired about my studies and nursing, the dances and the 'talent' in Armagh. As I left that summer evening, I felt something was amiss. I noticed aunt Mary's flushed face and dark circles under her eyes.

As I walked the short distance home, I hoped Paddy would return by Monday morning so we could catch up. I wanted to know if my boyfriend had been seen out with other girls. His red sports car drew them in. Despite his short height and lack of attractive looks, he was still my boyfriend since I was sixteen. He compensated for his lack of looks with his bubbly personality. Both of us enjoyed dancing and roller-skating sessions in our local Parochial Community Hall. Michael probably remained faithful because of the close community we come from. Someone would have whispered his infidelity to me in confidence, and he knew that. As a result of studying and working in the hospital most of the week, it was difficult to schedule dates. The nurses' training home where we lived prohibited boys from calling or staying out late on weekdays.

Michael vanished sometimes, too, especially on weekends when I came home unexpectedly. On that Friday night, a carnival dance was being held in a large tent near Ballymore crossroads, just a few miles out of town. According to rumours in Armagh, he had been seen there on other nights. A 'wee' nurse's aide also from Lisdonowen told my friend. Michael was nowhere to be found when I returned home.

Weekends off were not always guaranteed, and student nurses often filled in sick leave gaps on short notice. No date had been set with Michael. He usually noticed my car parked along the street just above our family's bicycle shop. Friday evening was winding down and we didn't have a phone at home. I never called him. I was wary of committing to Michael because he was older than me, had a string of broken relationships, and was known as a ladies' man. Despite the lack of a pact, we were known as a couple and had become faithful over time.

My mother was also unable to provide any information regarding Paddy. She would avoid eye contact when questioned about it, say that it was none of our business, now that he was a big lad, he would just show up when it suited him. Before swiftly moving the conversation on. I brought up the murder of the taxi driver. The crime shocked our community. Nodding at me without comment, her eyes averted to the stove where the tea was stewing. She seemed a bit agitated, so I wondered what was going on. While we ate her homemade apple pie and drank strong tea, the topic quickly shifted. She avoided talking about my Michael as well. Which was unusual. Typically, she would ask if he had seen me recently or mention if she had talked to him during the week. He would occasionally call in. When our friendship turned into a romantic relationship, she wasn't fully on board. With time, she grew to like him. My father was nine years older than my mother, and my mother considered Michael to be a sensible older boy. Leaving her free from the worry of other unsavoury or flighty relationships.

Saturday came and went. Neither Michael nor Paddy showed up. Michael was spotted, however. I saw him fly past in his sports car with a pretty girl through our shop window. As they turned at the Tee Junction, just opposite our home, they laughed and smiled at each other. I wondered who she was.

On Sunday, I grabbed Aunt Mary's arm as she scurried out of mass with me close behind her. As I was returning to Armagh soon, I asked if anything was wrong with Paddy's absence. She stopped and just stared past me. I was told that certain things could not be prevented, and I shouldn't worry about them. Suddenly, we noticed several women chatting and pointing in our direction. Mary pulled my arm and said, 'Come along with me for a cup of tea and leave those gossiping ninnies behind.'

We hurried towards the steps and the short distance to Mary's home. Lisdonowen was indeed small. During the week, Paddy was always in touch. In the nurses' training home there was only an incoming call phone. Paddy knew the number, but according to the nurses, he did not call. Neither did Michael. I didn't worry about Michael. I was simply curious about his antics. As Aunt Mary and I sat at the kitchen table, I gathered she would not tell me what had happened to Paddy. Michael was mentioned offhand, however. Since a cousin was staying at their family home, he was given the responsibility of taking her out. Mary seemed weary and sighed a lot, so I held back my curiosity, and she hugged me tightly before leaving and told me to enjoy my life. Her words were so pointed that I wondered why she expressed them that way.

Midweek, my mother called. She had to use our neighbour's phone, which was unusual for her. I was startled and prepared for the worst.

'He's okay,' she shouted down the phone as if we were thousands of miles apart. 'Your aunt asked me to let you know that Paddy has contacted her. There has been a very worrying incident, but he has not been injured. He has to lie low for a while. Disappear even. Your cousins aren't telling the whole story,' she babbled. 'They want you to keep it quiet. You must not talk to anyone about this. Talk is cheap and you don't know who is listening.'

By the conspiratorial way she spoke, it was as if we were living in England during the second world war. But this was only Northern Ireland. My hair stood up on the back of my neck as she talked. I heard the 'pips,' signalling the end of our conversation so we said our goodbyes quickly before the phone died. Michael, however, did show up again and eventually bought me a ring. We married in 1970 and have lived in Armagh with our own family ever since. Leaving behind that wee town and all its secrets. There have been a few more over the years. Michael rose through the ranks of the Civil Service while I nursed part-time. During 'The Troubles,' we endured bombings, killings, house searches, and military checkpoints. Always hoping for peace as the years passed in our contented way.

The best way to describe what happened to Paddy is that he disappeared. I never saw or heard from him again. While at home on leave, looking out the kitchen window at that favourite place of our youth, our sunny Grove, I imagined seeing the fairies dancing in a circle, laughing gleefully after they had stolen Paddy. He was truly 'away with the fairies. My cousins never told me what happened to him or where he was. They got better at keeping that secret over time.

'Never tell a secret.' My father used to say. 'Take it to the grave. If you tell one person, then it is no longer a secret. That person tells someone else, and it is gone.'

I rarely visited my aunt and uncle because travelling anywhere unnecessarily was troublesome and restrictive during those times. Especially to a border town. Home visits during daylight hours were short and sweet. Years after the disappearance, I did hear a story of sorts. I was caring for an elderly family friend who had been admitted to the ward.

'Patrick', he said, 'He got caught up in some bad business, don't you know. He was lifted by the police and did time. A bad business, too young a lad to get mixed up in other people's angsts. Those 'Stickies' 'auld IRA Officials. Men hankering after an 'all Ireland' at any cost.'
Those were the last words he said before writhing in chest pain never to recover.

He is alive and well today. Paddy. Just over the border

in County Louth, he lives among the Cooley Mountains. A perfect bachelor. Peter told me this when he saw me in the cobbled yard of the holiday home in Donegal when he visited. Paddy must be in his 60s like me. Weary of the world. Saddened by 'The Troubles' my heart skipped a beat hearing the true story unfolding.

In the late 1960s, sporadic 'Troubles' broke out all over the north. Disenchanted citizens marched for 'One Man, One Vote'. Fair wages and jobs for all. In its housing plan, the city council did not specify a preference for any one community or religion, but council housing in good areas was not often awarded to Catholics. When the UDR was formed, the official IRA resurfaced and carried out its 'legitimate' acts for 'the cause'. 'The Provos', the Provisional Irish Republican Army, was formed.

Paddy was swept up in the romance of it all. At seventeen, he was gullible and easily persuaded to join. But he never told me. His passion was for fair play. His job on that fateful August evening was to stand on the corner above the curve in the road leading to the bridge just outside the town as a 'lookout.' The men positioned themselves at the corner, where the bridge was hidden and waited for the taxi driver to approach. He was informed that his work was vital, and if anything were to happen, he would not be able to see it. Therefore, he could not be jailed. He was given an old railway train whistle to blow when he spotted the taxi. There was no mention that the man would die, only that he would be warned off. The men fled after shooting the taxi driver and crossed the Monaghan border into the south. They hid in a disused farmhouse that belonged to an IRA sympathiser. Police called the Murphy household to ask where their son was. Their home was being watched. Paddy quickly disappeared. Missing his mother's food. Missing the simple things in life. Missing me.

The murder was met with outrage from all sides. The RUC did not leave any stone unturned in their investigations, and everyone in our small town knew or guessed something. Paddy's possible location soon became the subject of much discussion and speculation in the local pub, which was notorious for its rumours and innuendo. His absence from home came to the fore.

The Murphy home was raided early one Sunday morning. A shocking intrusion into their lives. The entire house was turned upside down. In the room Paddy shared with his younger brother Peter, officers found a rusted and inactive gun. 'An Phoblacht', Republican news magazines, were found under the mattress. They were confiscated as evidence. Uncle John was taken to the Armagh Barracks, where he was questioned and kept for three nights, deprived of sleep, food and a solicitor. When he arrived home on Wednesday, battered and bruised, escorted by the police, he did not tell his family all the details. He had no information to share. Neither of the older men involved in the shooting came from our town. No one knew them. They used Paddy as a pawn. A little innocent, he had no idea of their real names or where they came from because of the secretive plot. Unbeknownst to him, a local woman had seen and identified him. From the window of her bungalow, she heard a shrill whistle and saw him blow it.

A few weeks later, under the cover of darkness, Paddy parked his bicycle in the entry and went into the kitchen by the back door, certain that no one had seen him. While Aunt Mary embraced him in tears, she pleaded with him to leave quickly, but it was too late. A group of armed police stormed into the house and took him by force, escorting him to the Saracen. He was also beaten and bruised when the family solicitor finally gained access to him in the Armagh Barracks. Paddy confessed to his involvement in that atrocity on that August evening, but after promises, he was given a light sentence because of his age. He had just turned seventeen. He was not able to give an accurate description of his comrades since they met at night. The lighting was always poor, and the fictitious names they used provided no value.

One of the first inmates at Long Kesh, the 'Maze' prison, Paddy began his ten-year sentence there. It was still early in the facility's development, and he was treated well. Most of the staff were recruited from England, so there were few prejudices. He served for only five years before getting out on good behaviour. He did not interact with paramilitary prisoners who were subsequently interned.

Secrets can be kept from family members especially. Even though others know about them. Assuming you already know, these unspoken things may never be retold to you. The only thing I knew about this was the garbled story of his need to disappear. My mother, father, brother, and sisters never told me the whole story. It was a secret they kept. Living in Armagh probably contributed to this. And I let it go. In the end, my thoughts about what happened were fairly accurate. I felt he was involved in some way. But I never thought he was a murderer.

The shock and shame of it all changed Paddy forever. After a long period of depression, he took up art again. There were art classes in prison. He excelled over time and became renowned for his art. In late 1974, he left Northern Ireland and settled in the Cooley Mountains of Southern Ireland. A local family that he befriended encouraged his artistic pursuits. Throughout his life, he held a few exhibitions in Dublin that brought him a nice little income. With the help of his lawyer, he successfully sued The Royal Ulster Constabulary (RUC) for undue force, ill-treatment, and injuries sustained during interrogation. With this, he was able to live a comfortable life. Despite this, his sisters continue to visit him regularly, and his brother Peter, who has a family and lives within walking distance, also visits often. He rides his bike the short distance to visit them. He rarely mentions that time but has recently inquired about me. Peter wants us to meet. Paddy would like to see me, he thinks. When we meet, I know we'll talk in our old frank and honest manner. Putting the world right. Reminiscing about the green Grove we used to play on when life was simple, and we were free.

The Low Road

Due to her parents' suspicions, Trina was not allowed to see her boyfriend. Both of us were thirteen, and Raymond, her boyfriend, was coming from Armagh to visit us in our wee border town 7 miles away. Raymond stood about a head above a crowd, and he always had to duck to get through doorways. He was incredibly handsome and charming, but he was fixated on her. We were both very excited. Likewise, I was smitten with him and jealous of their relationship.

It was planned that I would meet Raymond on The Low Road around 7 pm to explain why Trina couldn't see him. As I put on my Sunday best clothes and brand-new cream moccasins, my heart pounded.

I left the basement by the back door, mindful that everyone shouldn't see me, and tiptoed along the short lane to our meeting point. Slinking under the window of my uncle's home, sweat beading on my forehead I ran past the ball alley and under the railway bridge to The Low Road. Raymond was pacing in circles alongside the stream as I slowed down, panting and speechless. His cheeks lifted and his lips parted way with an uncontrollable smile as I approached, but as he looked beyond me, his expression darkened. He enquired where Trina was. He was devastated to learn that she couldn't make it.

'Is there any chance she will arrive later?' he asked. 'My lift won't arrive until nine.'

'No,' I replied.

'Please tell her I will call again at the usual time on Sunday, to the phone box near the post office.'

'Okay,' I stuttered whilst drinking in his chocolate almond-shaped eyes that held a lot of childish optimism and freckles that faintly dotted his cheeks but were only really visible in the sunshine. The way his shirt stretched taut around his shoulders when he shifted snagged and held my attention — I couldn't help but stare.

We chatted about school and the high jinks Trina, and I got into at the local youth club. While my mind floated off, imagining what it would be like to be his girlfriend, I knew in my heart that all he wanted to hear was about her. Instead, I foolishly hoped he would like me. That we had a chance while glancing down at my new cherished footwear.

As we made our way back along the Low Road that bright May evening, my heart began to race for fear that I would be seen. Conscious of my mother's casual but tight rein on us I was already thinking of a minefield of excuses to explain my absence. Despite this, I made it safely into our back garden without being noticed.

Seeing my mother's vegetable patch recently watered and then sodden cardboard spread over it to keep weeds at bay gave me the idea. To get suitably dirty, I lay on my side on the ground, avoiding marking my chic new moccasins. As I rubbed wet muck across the side of my face, I flipped the cardboard around my Sunday best skirt so that it looked wet. The plan was taking shape.

Trudging up the back stairs from the basement I could hear loud murmurs of conversation coming from the living room behind our bicycle shop. Feeling a surge of hope that the usual cèilidh house gathering was in full flow and I would arrive at the house unnoticed didn't happen. I stumbled on the last step. Unease suddenly slithered down my spine.

'Is that you?' my mother called out.

Muddy as if I had fallen, I stepped into the room and was greeted with a chorus of cries and sighs of, 'Thank god.' My heart sank. I knew then that I was really in for it. As she clouted me behind the ear with a wet dishcloth, my wise mother screamed.

'Explain yourself young lady and it better be good. How on earth did you get so muddy? Do you know it is after nine o'clock? We've been worried sick.'

To coax me into explaining, my gentle father stepped closer and put an arm around me. But when I finished fabricating the story, my older sister sarcastically interjected, 'Some story that. There are no big stones in our garden for you to trip over and be knocked unconscious for two hours. Tell another one.'

As accuser, jury, and judge, my mother began the inquisition and my sweet old uncle Tommy offered up the first clues to my disappearance. He saw me all dressed up and walking down The Low Road around 7 pm. While he didn't notice me returning, he did see that young man from Armagh walking up the street shortly after. The one that was courting wee young Neeley across the street.

'Too young, in my opinion, for such behaviour,' he replied.

I hated my uncle at that moment and for a very long time afterwards. I felt so betrayed. And so, it went on. Everyone chipping in their little bit. At last, my father intervened and slowly everyone dispersed. I was sent to bed. But it was not over yet.

Hot on my heels my mother followed me to the bedroom where my older sister and I slept. A more menacing tone filled her voice this time as she ranted and raved while my sister slouched behind her, listening closely to every word.

'You'll end up in a home. No one will want you. You will be taken to Middletown Convent, you heart scald you,' she screamed, meaning if I got pregnant. 'From now on you will come straight home from school and go to your room. You can only come down for your tea and then you will go straight back up. And, my fine lady, this will go on for as long as I see fit. I don't ever want to see you with that little trollop again. That Trina one.'

Crying was something I had long since stopped. I was

too often told that I cried constantly for the first three years of my life. Those tears returned that day, freed from their barrier.

I was sent to my room for what seemed like an eternity, day after day, week after week. Although I was also forbidden to chum around with Trina, we still managed to talk secretly from time to time in hidden places, away from my sister's prying eyes. Without her parents' knowledge, Trina continued to date Raymond.

Overcrowding in schools and a lack of workers for menial tasks in factories led the English government to lower the school leaving age the following year, so we left school at fourteen and drifted apart. Luckily, I managed to secure a local Pharmacy assistant job. My mother had no doubt asked on my behalf. While wearing the pharmacy's neat white fitted coat dress, I felt important for the first time. Once we donned our uniforms, we were all equal regardless of gender, age, or nationality — all simply pharmacists.

Over the next few months, I barely saw Trina or heard anything about her until we ran into each other on the street one day. Leaning in for our usual hug that carried on for far too long as we gushed about our lives. She looked a little pale and thin, so I was shocked when, babbling away, she announced that she was pregnant and expecting a child with her boyfriend Raymond but still had some months to go.

'I don't know how it happened,' she cried, rubbing her

eyes with the sleeve of her coat. 'I remember lying on a wall, we were kissing, and I was feeling drowsy. It must have happened then.'

I was speechless and struggled to swallow down a still-beating heart. Just then, I saw my sister flying out of our house, up the street.

'I must go, my tea will be ready,' I exclaimed.

'Cheerio,' Trina sadly replied, 'wish me luck.'

And so, I did, one hundred times and more to myself, before the day was over.

Hearing the chapel bells ring a few months later while filling a prescription at the pharmacy. I learned from the other Pharmacy assistant that there was a wedding in town. A young girl from the area was getting married.

'Who?' I asked, 'is it anyone that I might know?'

'Yes, it's Trina Neeley. She's only fourteen and is expecting a baby, don't you know her? I heard you were friends once,' she added.

Mumbling that I needed to go to the toilet, I excused myself and swiftly headed for the bathroom, where I promptly burst into tears. Part of me did not understand, but deep down I knew exactly what had happened. I recalled my mother's reaction on that fateful day when I disappeared down The Low Road. Even then, I understood why my mother was being so harsh.

From an ancient book called, the facts of life, interwoven with stories about God and his mother Mary, the Sacred Heart Nuns taught me about birds and bees. Before those convent closed-door sessions with Mother Jude constantly blushing as she read to us, I already knew the facts. During a visit to a friend's uncle's farm, Mary explained exactly how cows make and give birth to calves, much as humans do.

Life continued as usual after that. Trina gave birth to a baby. A little girl. The next year, while expecting her second child, Trina and Raymond moved out of Trina's parents' home.

During the late 1960s, rumours spread that civil rights marches were taking place across Northern Ireland demanding an end to discrimination against the Catholic minority. Northern Ireland's first civil rights march was held on August 24th, 1968. Many more marches would be held over the following year. Loyalists attacked some of the marches and organized counter-demonstrations to get the marches banned. Bernadette Devlin, a young university student, began appearing more frequently on television.

Bernadette became a People's Democracy activist and the youngest woman ever elected to Westminster. As a family, we became interested in her political views. My father was a strong supporter of politics throughout his life. As children, we heard him, and his friends speak openly and affirmatively about the 1916 Rising. As I grew to understand the significance of the changes now occurring in Northern Ireland, I began asking my father more questions about politics. He told me that his brother Dan served in the Irish Republican Army (IRA) in the twenties, and had he been older at the time, he would have probably joined as well.

The Troubles began when the UVF carried out three attacks on Catholics in Belfast. In the first, a Protestant civilian died when UVF members tried to firebomb the Catholic-owned pub beside her house but accidentally struck her home. In the second, a Catholic civilian was shot dead as he walked home. In the third, the UVF opened fire on three Catholic civilians as they left a pub, killing one and wounding the other two. In retaliation, fires were deliberately set ablaze in Orange Halls throughout the countryside, where sections of the Protestant community socialised, held dances, and practised marching band music. Those incidents shocked us all to the core. It was the late 1960s. Soldiers and patrols routinely patrolled the streets but despite the mayhem and chaos, life continued.

Around the same time, I left our wee town and Trina behind to train as a psychiatric nurse in Armagh, where I lived most of the week. As I listened to the news one day, I was shocked to hear that my hometown's small, no longer used protestant school was engulfed in fire one day. Sadly, the fire claimed the life of a young married father of two from the area. A local man was believed to have started the fire. Police were not looking for anyone else. That young man was Raymond, Trina's husband, and father of her two beautiful children. Nurse training made it difficult for me to visit Trina then to console her. Visitors to a home or funeral of a known Republican were scrutinized for possible IRA sympathies, so it was also potentially dangerous. Furthermore, there would be TV cameras with reporters. 1967 was the year. We were all nervous.

During a lunch break in the nurse's quarters, I saw Trina, her pitiful figure with their two young children on the news as the funeral cortège walked by with the coffin draped in the Irish tricolour. The tiny screen was filled with what appeared to be the whole town walking proudly behind the coffin. A black and white film as large as life.

Trina and I met by chance not that long ago. She looked very much the same with her beautiful classic looks, porcelain skin, high cheekbones, and gorgeous wide brown eyes. Like me, she had some wrinkles, but they weren't as deep-set as mine. We were both now in our sixties. As we talked, the years melted away.

'I have lost two husbands. Both because of The Troubles and look at you. You've led a charmed life.'

If only she knew.

Twelfth Night

Especially on weekends, when we were off duty. A few of the nursing students would attend dances anywhere and everywhere. It was at the height of the '60s. 'Flower Power,' drugs, and dancing. As dancing enthusiasts from outside Armagh City, we had always had a blast. To dance was freedom.

There was no one to censure us. No older siblings to squeal on us as we danced our way around the county and beyond, Edendork, Dungannon, Cookstown and of course The Armagh City Hall.

Occasionally, dances were held on Saturday evenings, especially in July in the Orange Hall, an Ulster Protestant venue located along the left side of The Armagh City Mall. This particular part of the city and the hall were considered 'no go' zones for us. We were Catholics. It was on the wrong side of the divide where we were frequently labelled the colourful moniker 'Taig'.

Breda, Maura, and I were best friends. Always up for the 'craic'. One fine summer evening, Breda, the daredevil, suggested we attend the Twelfth of July dance at The

Orange Hall. Flabbergasted, we thought, how on earth could or would we go there?

Protestants celebrated 'Orange' day on this date commemorating Protestant King William of Orange's victory over Catholic King James II at the Battle of the Boyne: a pivotal moment for the Protestant cause. Historically, it was a day that had seen outbursts of violence between the two sides.

If we get past the ticket booth, what then? That was my first thought. Other protestant nursing colleagues may be going, and someone would surely recognise one of us as a 'Taig'. Most of us have gotten to know one another over the past few years and have made it a point to be aware of where each of us hails from. This is a small town. A 'wee' city. Breda however had a foolproof plan, which she sold to us. The timing was crucial to the plan. To make it work, we were assured we needed a little vodka first. It was not only to relax us but to also demonstrate that we were carefree celebrators of 'The Twelfth'.'

Don't wear any holy crosses or pioneer pins,' she instructed. 'And be careful about what you say, especially your name and where you're from. Make it up as you go.' All hyped up and ready to have a good time, we walked from the hospital into town at the agreed time of 9 pm.

We arrived at the Beresford Hotel after passing a few drunken revellers peeing and singing slurred snippets of 'The Sash My Father Wore' behind a low wall. The hotel just outside the city centre was located in a neutral area.

It had an open policy. All customers are welcome. As long as you spend lots of money, there is no colour or religious discrimination. When we reached the hotel, we were greeted with loud music and dancing in the foyer and were quickly roped into a highland fling-type dance in which we were swung around by our partners. Arms locked in a similar style to 'Ceilidh' dancing. For several rounds, we enthusiastically participated, occasionally letting out a yelp before we moved on to the bar.

Most of the crowd was more than a little drunk near the bar area, where the standing room was limited. The mix of reds and blues in our miniskirt outfits helped us blend in. Agreeing with everyone who asked, that we had a great time at the Twelfth parades we slipped in among the crowd and made a beeline for the bar to order modest mixers. These we topped up, out of sight, with the vodka Maura had snuck in her bag.

A young, attractive man with a manly, peppered stubble struck up a conversation with me. Seeing that he wasn't too intoxicated, Breda nudged and whispered in my ear to ask if he was going to the dance. As I sipped the vodka mix that was way too strong but helped the dregs of the day to wear off the young man with a devil-may-care outlook and stellar smile invited us all to accompany him. We learned later that this was another part of the plan coming together. We were all set.

On leaving the hotel, our new friend's two male companions joined. Tipsier than him they, all the same, looked handsome in their band kilts and jackets. They were a flicker with curiosity and genial smiles. As we weaved our way through the town and up to The Mall, where the dance hall was nestled among magnificent Georgian houses, we cut a colourful dash. All dressed in red, white, and blue.

On approaching the Orange Hall, Maura whispered in my ear,

'So far, so good.'

In the heart of the city, surrounded by the tall Georgian houses, The Mall was a picturesque grassy expanse flanked by two museums, a GP's office, a church and The Orange Hall on one side of it. A racetrack in Victorian times, The Mall was fenced off on the outside. Along with the open spaces in the central area, smaller paths ran vertically, interspersed with coarse wooden benches. Now a fine cricket pitch stood in its midst in front of a low red-brick cricket club. The graceful tree-lined mall was dotted with many artistic structures, including a war memorial.

In the sixties, boyfriends used to pay for their girlfriends' dance tickets. They usually paid for the entire evening's drinks and meals as well. There was one downside however to the unspoken agreement, as the men expected to leave you home, kiss them and perhaps engage in more. As we paired off, walking towards The Orange Hall, it looked like another part of the plan seemed to be falling into place. The ticket booth was no longer a concern.

We danced the night away to a young Scottish band covering all the current hits by Sandy Shaw, Lu Lu, The Royal Show Band, etc., on a dance floor filled with young people, occasionally nipping off to the lady's room to top up our vodka. To delay our return to our new male friends, we jived and boogied to the 'Hippy Hippy Shake' and 'The Twist' with others and trusted that no one would relay news of our clandestine outing to our catholic boyfriends. We were all grins, dancing like no one was watching like it was our last night on Earth. It could have been just our minds avoiding thinking about the hangover to come. Inside we're just happy, happy and more alive than ever.

As we huddled in the lady's room one last time to polish off the vodka, we discussed our exit strategy. 'God Save The Queen' would end the dance at midnight. We needed to leave as soon as the band went quiet, and each member stood in line at the front of the stage to perform the British national anthem. Knowing our escorts would most likely stand at attention during that time we made a pact to dash out separately and meet halfway across The Mall at the war memorial statue.

Hearts thumping, we burst through the doors into the artificial glow of streetlamps and ran across the street, reaching the war memorial within a few minutes. We could hear the rendering of 'God Save the Queen' and a roar at the end. With a good vantage point, although partially hidden behind ancient gangly trees, it was close enough to hear. The doors of the dance hall, which had earlier been closed and guarded, burst open.

First to fall out was my new acquaintance, followed closely by his two friends wobbling. We could hear the angry words.

'For feck's sake where did they go, those bitches! What a waste of time. Thought I was all set with that wee ginger one,' the boy I was with, yelled.

'Oh,' his friend Robert slurred back. 'Think I saw that wee ginger-headed one before may be down at the hospital. I noted the hair when she gave me grandad a cup of tea. Typical Taig if you ask me. Catholic to the core. I think we've been had from the word go, boys.'
Just then, the boys were swallowed up by the surging crowds leaving the hall and beginning to cross The Mall. It was time to go. We hurried off, but not too fast, hoping not to attract attention. Running towards the hospital and the nurses' home in the charcoal of almost-dawn laughing and giggling all the way.

As we continued our training, time passed quickly. 'The Troubles' impacted our lives both inside the hospital, nursing broken hearts and minds, as well as outside of it. Those years will forever remain a central part of our memories.

Now and then, I wonder where Breda is. She left unexpectedly after she trained, to go to England. Some years later, I was informed that she was pregnant and had given up her baby. That I will never know for sure. Before she left, she looked as if she had put on a lot of weight. Another old friend said she moved to Dublin to work as a nurse, that she married a nice young Protestant male nurse, had twin daughters, and never returned to Northern Ireland-Maura, sadly passed away at a young age. Our friendship had endured, meeting regularly with our families, and sharing stories of our past. Her love of vodka had taken its toll on her. For years, I watched her slug it out of her handbag. Never sober and often drunk.

Our friendship through those troubled years remains cherished, and I will never forget that Twelfth night. Whenever I walk around The Mall, I look over at The Orange Hall, remembering those carefree days of innocence, fun, and laughter. The crazy fun times. Music, friends, good times, dance.

There is No Flag Worth Dying For

On Duty

As I stepped past the bicycles and tried not to get grease on my neat blue nurse's uniform, I heard a soft low noise coming from the direction of our shop. The lighting was poor. On the far side of the counter was a display window filled with bicycle tyres, tubes, and other parts making the space bereft of the early Autumn morning light. The blanket of night barely lifted.

This Monday morning was Nurses' Pupil Training School, where we would be assigned our shifts on the wards. It was essential to be on time for the seven-thirty handover report. As I lifted my basket over the handlebars and saddles, I could feel the weight of its contents. Food sneaked out of cupboards from home to eke out my allowance for the weeks ahead whilst I lived in the nurse's training digs in Armagh.

When I first heard the noise, I assumed that cross old Peg was snoring amid the bicycles. Peg, the dog of our elderly neighbour, was prone to chasing us and snapping at our ankles before suddenly stopping and falling into a deep slumber. As I neared the front door, the low sound became intermittent.

We rarely locked our front door. The local community was close, and there were no outward signs of threat or fear. On occasion, it was bolted if the whole family was attending a wedding or funeral. With the family spreading its wings, we rarely went on holidays or attended functions together anymore. Invariably, the door was left ajar. The door of the shop past the gleaming new bicycles was also the entrance to the rest of our home.

The house consisted of a large living room cum kitchen connected to the shop front, with a basement below the house where my father used to fix bicycles, radios, and later TVs. Several large sash windows and fireplaces adorned the three bedrooms upstairs. Perfect for the long dark winter months. In the backyard, there was a large toilet room below the loft that was part of the outhouses.

The shop was once a pub before my parents bought it in the 1940s. My father had a passion to fix things and make broken objects workable or better again. It was possibly his passion that inspired me to become a nurse, the desire to help others and make them better. With its dark panelled wood fronted counter and shelving, the open space of the pub made it easy to transform it into a bicycle shop. The only evidence that it was once a pub was two Guinness pumps. Still in situ hidden behind an old bubble amber-stained glass partition.

I doubled back to check the Battery House and concluded that cross old Peg with her big floppy ears was snoring. The Battery House was a walk-in closet off the hallway. It had the same type of amber-bubbled glass as the back of the shop. My father used this space to charge car batteries for locals as a way to earn some extra money for our keep. The pub probably used it to store cigarettes and drinks at one time that had been smuggled across the border a few miles away. Definitely snoring, I repeated to myself, as I gingerly opened the door to the Battery House. Unexpectedly, I spotted a young, long, lanky soldier dressed in a pale khaki uniform and boots. Leaning on the shelves in dreamland with his rifle slung over his right shoulder. Even in his relaxed state, his pose held power. He did not stir.

The feeling of animosity toward English soldiers wasn't present in Northern Ireland yet. Recently deployed to Ulster, they were accepted as our saviours. We learned of their arrival through newspaper clips and newsreels at the cinema along with images of them taking tea from residents across the Falls Road in Belfast. Their purpose was to resolve 'The Troubles.'

During the night, it had rained in generous water pellets, and I could feel the chill of Autumn in the hall. Poor thing, I thought as I stared at his handsome tanned face with square jawline and pitied his night shift. Closing the door quietly I left. Leaving him to arouse on his own.

As I stepped towards the chink of light coming through the slightly ajar front doors, I hoped my car, a sporty-looking Triumph Herald, would start and that I had enough petrol. Slipping out the front door, I closed them gently too. As no one else was up around at 6.30 am, I knew he wouldn't be disturbed, at least not yet.

Despite the obvious damage to the Triumph Herald, my father and I decided to purchase it. It had been written off by the insurance company. My mother instructed us to look for a car so that I could return home on weekends. When we saw it by the garage outside of town, it was a heap of broken pieces. Despite the Triumph's workings being set aside at the wall, we could still see its potential and both believed it could be restored to its former glory. Having brought the Triumph to life, it was parked a little up the sloped street from our shop behind our neighbour's immaculate green Ford Anglia. The Triumph lacked a good mechanic's touch though as the hand brake wasn't functioning properly, so it was unreliable. But I still loved it.

As soon as I was sure no one was watching, I leaned my car forward to touch the bumper of my neighbour's car. In this way, I could back up and move out using the reverse gear. The Fiesta's shiny bumper showed no sign of dents from my furtive use, and my neighbour was, hopefully, unaware of its illicit use.

It was about seven miles to Armagh. Going out of town, there was little traffic, so I hoped it would be clear. I wanted to arrive early for the ward on-duty handover report. Sadly, this was not the case. About halfway there, near the crossroads, I spotted an army checkpoint in the distance. God, will we ever get used to this checking, car searching, questions, questions, questions? I pondered. There was already a line of cars in front and each one was being searched. As I slid up to the barrier, I hoped I would be waved through. Suddenly, my thoughts turned to the soldier in our battery house. Has he awakened for his handover of duty, or has he continued to snore his way through the morning?

My car was the next to be searched but the officer waved me through. As I sped off glad that the checkpoint had let the nurses' uniform swing in my favour, I reflected again on the sleeping soldier. With a few minutes to spare, my thoughts turned back to work and the shift that lay ahead of me. Hoping all would go well, I dashed off to the ward.

It wasn't until a few family members gathered around our house one weekend months later that I remembered the young soldier snatching forty winks. Chatting over several cups of tea, Dermot the barber and his wife, our neighbours reminisced about the Second World War. The story of a US platoon of soldiers and pilots stationed near the border of Northern Ireland. My father recounted the story of the American for the umpteenth time. It was murky that morning. He awoke early to a noise in the shop. Hearing a low snoring sound, he discovered a young US Officer, a pilot, in full uniform in the battery house, asleep while standing. Knowing that his colleagues would miss him, my father woke him up.

On that early August morning, I shared my experience

of the snoring English soldier. We marvelled at the coincidence. Later that evening, I worried about his safety. It was not a foreign war these soldiers were serving in, but rather our Troubles that would escalate for many years to come.

Years later, while renovating our family home, my brother Arthur found a US Pilot cap badge lying between the wooden steps to our old basement. He guessed it belonged to that American pilot my parents had befriended.

The young pilot who became a frequent visitor would sit with my father down in the basement while he repaired bicycles and old radios conversing over war and life stories. Near the end of the war, he was recalled to his unit one day to fly his Warhawk over Germany on a bombing mission. We never heard from him again.

Recently, Arthur donated a US Air Force cap badge to the War Museum in Armagh, where it resides with a printed card explaining its history. I often wonder whether the two young men sleeping in our battery house survived their tours of duty decades apart.

The Wake

Noreen was devastated when she heard the news. Her beloved husband was fatally shot at an Army checkpoint outside Armagh.

When we first met, Noreen and I were nursing elders with dementia of varying degrees in ward six. She was a very attractive and efficient state-enrolled nurse with deep brown eyes and warm chestnut colour hair. When she smiled and laughed you couldn't help but smile along too. We were informed of Noreen's arrival in advance through the nurse's grapevine. According to reports, Noreen was engaged to a farmer who lived in the country outside of town. Their romance began in their early teens.

I was the staff nurse in charge the evening she arrived on the ward. We weren't all that different in age and I hoped we could get along well. The staff praised her work ethic. She was punctual, trustworthy plus caring and friendly with the patients, yet private about her personal life. We became more acquainted as the months passed. Later in the year, we were assigned to the same duty schedule. A rotation of twelve weeks once a year. Some of the night shift nurses couldn't get along without friction. Fortunately, we got along very well. As we lived close to each other, we were able to share lifts and had the freedom to discuss both personal and everyday matters. There was something in the way she smiled, a warmth, a genuineness, a softness of spirit I just couldn't pass up.

One evening, as Noreen and I travelled to work, she announced that her wedding plans were postponed. She was uncertain about marrying her fiancé.

'Barney keeps asking me to set a date, Sarah. We have been together since leaving school and I feel our relationship has become a habit,' Noreen timidly revealed. 'He is a very kind and caring man, but I'm not convinced that we are really compatible. Eventually, he will inherit his family's farm, which he cherishes but all he wants to discuss is this cow or pig, or the price of lambs at the market, and his parents expect us to live on the farm in an annexe. This doesn't appeal to me.'

Noreen was a very worldly woman, so this didn't surprise me. When off duty, she was always pushing the boundaries with the latest 1970s styles. But that always flattered her. An incredibly beautiful woman with a pair of arched eyebrows, delicate ears that framed an elegant nose and a sculpted figure which was twine-thin to match. When the nurses' association held their monthly disco in the hospital recreation hall, she attended without her fiancé. She had a passion for dance which she flowed in and was excellent at The Twist and Jive. I wondered if she and Barney were compatible. On those short trips to and from Armagh City Hospital, and during those long night shifts, she grew wistful and depressed, talking about her inner anxieties and worries. Misery was written all over her face.

On our return to day duty, we were pleased to be back on the same nursing team with only occasional changes in our shift schedules. Despite our friendship blossoming on night duty, Norah became guarded and rarely mentioned Barney during our days together. She grew a little distant, quietly carrying out the tasks we were administered for the day in a slower, cumbersome way.

To meet the ward's needs, the nursing sister sent different levels of staff on their breaks together, so we were not able to catch up as often during the day. During our occasional meals together in the canteen, I began to notice a gradual but positive shift in her mood. There was a twinkle in her eyes. Less preoccupied and broody, she was suddenly more talkative, discussing recent dances she had attended in bubbly tones. She walked with a bounce. I guessed she had decided about her wedding date.

As I was rushing home one Saturday to take off the little one since his granny wasn't available, I saw Noreen hop into a stylish green and white Mini. The driver was not Barney. I lingered for a while, pretending to look for my car keys in the basket I carried to work. She was giggling and laughing as the man leaned in to kiss her. I finally understood why Noreen seemed so much happier, but I wasn't sure who this new person was. It was a rare early summer's day. The sky blazed blue. The sun a celebration of yellow, free and bright, and I felt some sense of recognition. Dating him would not be a good idea if he were whom I suspected. He was dubbed 'The Armagh Guevara' by the media. In the news for all the wrong reasons. His terrorist career was featured almost every week in The Irish News. As part of his evasive activities, he regularly hopped across manned border areas just several miles away, from Armagh, to take potshots at soldiers. Those free state borders Monaghan and Castleblaney in Southern Ireland.

Mr Robinson a prominent politician from Northern Ireland, famously crossed into the small Monaghan village of Clontibret from a border near Armagh with a group of loyalists in opposition to the recently signed Anglo-Irish Agreement. An area that provided unrestricted travel along the border. During the incursion, they proceeded to vandalise many buildings in the village and beat up two police officers before being dispersed by the Garda Síochána. All of the invaders made it back over the border except Peter Robinson, who was arrested and spent the night in a Republic of Ireland gaol, making headlines. The same border area they crossed over from was also a convenient escape route for active dissident republicans and was regularly used for smuggling goods such as bombs and arms. It demonstrated to the English political world how easy it was to access what was then known as 'The Free State'.

'The Armagh Guevara's' real name and address were known by most Catholics in the city. Back then, word of mouth was extremely powerful. He was Noreen's new flame. The same flame that leapt over a wall across from our home and started a gun battle with Soldiers as I fled to safety pushing our baby's pram. I decided to approach her regarding her new beau after learning of numerous sightings of him through other nurses. We were friendly enough to have that dialogue. I was concerned that she might not know his reputation. Sean's large extended family was Republican. He joined the Irish National Liberation Army (INLA) in his early twenties.

Noreen was unexpectedly transferred to a different ward that was short-staffed, so I missed the opportunity to converse with her. We had touched on the subject of her new romance while she glanced around the room and behind her. As she grew distant, I knew she sensed my disapproval. She avoided any exchange that touched on her new relationship. We no longer travelled together because we were on opposite shifts and slowly lost contact as the days, months, and years passed. According to the grapevine, she had married Sean and moved to a new housing complex out of town. Soon after, she gave birth to a daughter. My life also moved on. As our family grew, we moved house several times. I resigned from my job when we had our fourth child, a little girl. The decision seemed logical.

Many months later when my mother and older sister

arrived on one of their fortnightly visits. I could sense their excitement as I opened the hall's inner door. They were on a mission. Knowing how much I loved working as a nurse, they informed me that a local hospital was in the early stages of closing some of its acute admission wards and moving the services to a newly built hospital ten miles away.

The new general hospital would have a purpose-built Early Treatment Unit attached to it. An open ward to treat patients with early mental health issues. This was a new concept. Local newspaper ads were placed to recruit staff. Due to the daily reports of horrific bombings and shootings, they knew I didn't read the local news often, so they wanted to share this exciting news. The new unit required night staff and was offered two nights of part-time work per week. As they sipped their tea and told me this, I could see the joy and delight in their eyes. It was exciting news, indeed. With little interruption to our family life, I could return to my beloved job. Several months later, I was hired.

The trip to the new job would have its challenges with roadblocks and searches. Nevertheless, I quickly got over my apprehension about leaving our local area for relatively safe travel. I attended several induction sessions at the new unit and was delighted to find that several other nurses from Armagh, nurses I knew well, had also been hired as part-time night staff. In the hope of safety in numbers, the Armagh nurses put together a travel plan at our local hotel for those ten fraught miles. Companionship would not only give the trip an air of safety, but it would also be cost-effective. With four, night shift wards, each requiring two staff members, we were able to frequently share lifts between at least two or three nurses from Armagh. A mix of staff nurses enrolled nurses and assistant nurses. After many tweaks, we were confident that the plan would work.

As one of the car owners, I was pleasantly surprised to discover that one of my travelling companions was Noreen. We hadn't talked for years, but we quickly re-established our friendship. Noreen and several other nurses lived in the rapidly growing suburbs of the city, so we arranged a meeting place for the pick-up. Across from the imposing Armagh Courthouse, there was an accessible parking lot near the centre of town. It was also close to the Portadown road that led to the hospital. An ideal meeting point since drivers could safely pull over and meet passengers who made their way there.

From time to time, travel companions changed due to holidays or illness. At least two or three people were typically on the same rotation, working the same two-night shifts every week. We chatted freely about our daily worries and tensions on our way to work. Upon reflection, I remember that Noreen kept the discussion very general, mainly talking about her young daughter and extended family. Her disclosures were carefully controlled. Rarely mentioning Sean. We all knew his reputation. He was known to have spent long periods away from his home evading the security forces.

As we settled into a routine of travelling to work, the weeks, months, and years passed by quickly. The many roadblocks and occasional scary events became the norm. We were young then and all of this had become a way of life. In general, wearing our nurse's uniforms allowed us to get to work quickly and safely. Although not always.

During one particular evening, we were stopped at a road check just outside the city on our way to the hospital. After waiting for a long time, we were told to move on. When probed, a friendly UDR Soldier and neighbour of one of the girls whispered the news to us.

'A shooting took place beyond the other side of town and rumours say that at least two people were killed, leading to the closure of all exit and entrance roads into the city.'

Instinctively, we knew that wasn't the whole story. Most likely, the lockdown was set up before the shooting. Security forces were probably on a mission to prevent potential bombings or shootings by known dissidents.

Our conversation ceased as we grappled with this information. We quietly prayed. Noreen's quiet sobbing broke the silence. Her sobbing was as if she could bleed an ocean from her eyes. As she tried to catch her breath in the back seat, we could sense her daily anguish. We all knew Sean's reputation and his deeds. We had no words to comfort her. Marie, who sat next to her, wrapped her arms around her and helped her settle down as we moved off, leaving us late for work once more. Each of us wondered silently what had really happened.

Noreen was nowhere to be seen the following morning, to travel with us back to Armagh. We waited quite some time for her in the parking lot. On occasion, the morning report could take longer than usual, or the day staff would be delayed arriving at work, so we were not overly concerned that she was running late. Upon seeing the night nursing officer approaching quickly along the path, we knew something was wrong.

Our hearts sank as she told us that Noreen was taken home by a family member in the early morning. Her husband was dead, executed alongside another young man from Armagh near the Clontibret border. We were in shock. Matron had no further information to share. Before moving on we let the painful news of the tragedy sink in and then slowly made our way home filled with sadness. Every few miles we were met with checkpoints, making us late to relieve some of our worried husbands so they could leave for work on time.

The wake took place at Noreen and Sean's home almost a week after the shooting when his remains were released from the hospital. The burial date was postponed due to forensics and formal inquiries regarding the shooting. Another nursing colleague, Lizzy, from a Protestant background, insisted on going with me to the wake. I knew she was nervous due to her background and affiliations. Even though I was apprehensive for her, I did not voice it. She was a close friend.

We duly went, to attend the second evening of the wake. Crowds of mourners blocked the roadway near Noreen's home as they spilt out onto the surrounding pavement of the housing estate. So, we parked some distance away and walked up a hilly avenue, past two occupied Land Rovers parked discreetly on a sloped corner between hedges. As we approached the wake, we passed groups of men pacing around smoking cigarettes while speaking in hushed tones. The women were probably providing tea and some comfort to Noreen in her home.

A few older men wandered slowly through the crowd in an authoritative manner, occasionally looking down toward the police. It was evident they were aware of their presence. The men appeared to be 'some of the boys', attentive, ready to alert those on wanted lists or on the run to the police presence. Bin lids crashed and banged in the distance, alerting residents to the possibility of an impending raid in their area.

We walked through the thronged hallway into the wake room. In a calm and relaxed manner, Noreen rose from her vigil chair beside the coffin, hugged each of us and thanked us for coming. Considering it was the second day of the wake, Noreen was probably numb and tired.

Traditionally, Irish wakes keep the coffins open. In the silken-covered burial box, a cascade of mass cards would accumulate around the deceased, whose hands would be clasped in prayer with a string of rosary beads draped over them. This coffin was closed.

Sean's body was rendered unrecognisable after he was shot multiple times that fateful night. Noreen's nursing friends had never met Sean. Except for me, on the day he initiated the exchange of fire with Soldiers from the wall in Irish Street over me and my little one in his pram. They nevertheless saw his face in the Local Gazette, along with that of his companion who was also gunned down that evening. He looked older than he was in the 1980s newspaper reports as it was now the fifteenth year of The Troubles. That bland description of the war.

A framed picture from an earlier time was placed on top of the coffin. The long curly hair and neat suit of the seventies, along with his youthful innocence, were mesmerising. Taking us aside, Noreen led us to their little girl's room. During this stressful time, we knew Anna May would be with her grandparents. My thoughts kept drifting back to what could have happened to our young infant when Sean was on his shooting spree in 1971 as we sat on that little bed hugging and reminiscing.

We promised to keep in touch and as we got ready to leave, she informed us of the details of the funeral times the following day. I let Lizzy go first as we stepped out of the little room. I had very negative thoughts about Sean. As I embraced Noreen, again, I couldn't help but say what was rankling in my heart,

'Noreen I am here for you only. Not him.'

Recoiling at my words, she gave me a scornful look, visibly biting her lower lip as I quickly left. Lizzy was unaware of our exchange. She was more concerned about leaving and getting home as quickly as possible. As we pushed our way through the mourners arriving and departing and the press loitering down the road, her discomfort became more apparent.

The following day, I did not attend Sean's large funeral. I had no desire to go. However, Lizzy and the other nurses with whom we travelled went. Her attendance surprised me. She seemed to stand out on Ulster TV's live news broadcast. Maybe I was the only one who noticed her. Thousands followed the sad procession to the Cathedral for the funeral mass. Photographers and journalists were in abundance. I learned many years later that Lizzy's husband worked part-time for the UDR at that time.

Noreen returned to night duty after a time. Despite showing up for her lifts, she was much quieter than usual. As we avoided discussing Sean, our conversations became fragmented and stilted. We were at a loss for words. The months and years rolled by as we travelled back and forth to the hospital. Eventually, Noreen contemplated leaving nursing and was hired as a part-time school nurse at the school her fast-growing daughter attended a short distance from their home.

To keep herself busy, Noreen also worked two weekly nights of duty. This filled up her lonely days. How she managed it, we don't know. She was dropped off at her school after night duty shifts. We wanted to be kind to her, so we went out of our way, often arriving at our own homes late after dropping her off. Noreen quickly became accustomed to our assistance and scolded us when we couldn't meet her schedule. Although this wasn't a problem for us as we understood her desire to keep busy.

Soon after, a handsome young staff nurse was assigned to night duty, and he began chatting freely with Noreen. We noticed how her eyes began to sparkle again and how she easily laughed in his presence while touching his shoulder. Her close friends around her gave her great comfort, however, I always felt that she didn't feel the same way about me. From the outside, we seemed to get along, but she never revealed that she was in a serious relationship with Kevin, the male nurse. I guessed it was happening. Noting the frequency, the two would often have supper together at the staff canteen. The way she smiled when they met. The whole unit was abuzz with excitement.

Due to our distanced relationship, I was the last nurse to learn of Noreen's engagement and plans to move to New Zealand with Kevin. We were all a little shocked but delighted for her. Their wedding date, visa, and passage to New Zealand were all set. Sadly, I was not invited to the big event. It hurt. Knowing that those words that I said to her at the wake were never forgiven. Despite knowing that it would have been discussed, none of the other nurses mentioned it to me. It was difficult to find the right wedding gift for them. I settled on a nicely framed photo of all the Armagh nurses who travelled through those many journeys through those times together. I later learned she took it to New Zealand with her.

We heard little snippets of Noreen's life abroad over the years. Her daughter grew into a beautiful young woman with good looks favouring her father, Sean. Kevin and Noreen never had children together but they both secured jobs as nurses and enjoyed the sunny lifestyle in their new adopted country.

The strain of those night duty years began to take its toll on me. Following a serious infection that required surgery, I decided to resign from my job. When the first treatment didn't work, I realised my resistance was low and handed in my notice. After several months of regaining my strength and subsequent successful surgery, I knew I had made the right decision to take a break.

After eight years, Noreen, Kevin, and Anna May returned to Ireland. The news of Noreen's illness shocked us all. Her habit of smoking twenty cigarettes a day did not help. In addition to breast cancer, she had lung cancer. Tragically, she was dying.

Our neighbours and friends from across the street were celebrating their wedding anniversary and invited my husband and me. Noreen's uncle Damian had a history of cancer in his family. He lost his 20-year-old brother to the disease. As we entered our friends' house, I briefly wondered if Noreen would be there, but did not see her.

We congratulated her aunt May and Damian, who insisted we share a glass of red wine with them. As Mick and I wandered around the room, I noticed Noreen coming in through the back door. My old travelling companion. My heart leapt as she smiled at me and put her arm through mine. All those years that she felt distant melted away. She led us out into the sunlit yard, and I stared into the deep brown eyes with the long black eyelashes that framed them, but I was more drawn to the circles below them. Once sallow, her skin now appeared a deep yellow and her once shapely body was now frail and thin. As she lit a cigarette and inhaled deeply, she began sputtering and coughing.

'Should you be doing that?' I said without thinking.

As she laughed, I knew she had forgiven me for my candour. And for those pointed words at the wake. Words I had spoken to her while leaving Sean's wake all those years ago. She pulled me closer as we walked back through the years together.

'It doesn't matter now,' she said about her smoking habits.

Sharing how little time the doctor predicted she had left. As she sat with me for most of the evening, I felt a mix of anguish and happiness. I knew I was truly forgiven. Maybe she had heard the story of Sean's reckless behaviour in our street long ago.

I couldn't go to her wake or her funeral. I knew I wouldn't be missed. Funerals are something I tend to avoid. I spent most of her burial day, with a lump in my throat trying to blink away the tears. Thinking about her, and Sean's wake as well. Reminiscing about Lizzy and her secrets, our nursing friends, and our journeys to the hospital, sometimes fraught with danger.

Kevin, Noreen's husband, remarried within a few years of her death. Her beautiful daughter lives in Armagh now, a short distance from where she spent her childhood. She is married to a practising Solicitor and has two children. Anna May is friendly with my daughter with whom she enjoys discussing me and her mother's friends. She comments on the kindness of the nurses who gave her lifts to work all those years ago. Knowing these things, I feel in my heart that Noreen passed along only the best memories of her friends, during her troubled life, to her daughter. My quiet and pointed words to her at the wake were understood, in time, as Sean's illicit activities were reported in the media. Those revelations form part of our troubled history and are banked in our minds forever.

Legitimate Target

'You're still a target, Keeley!' Aldo jokingly shouted up the street, as they both tumbled out of the pub after hours.

During the mid-1980s, events in Northern Ireland had taken an unexpected turn. People were singled out, shot at their homes, and blown up in their cars, pubs, and workplaces. People with Paramilitary, police and Army connections were all at risk. All sides were fighting for control.

Ivan, Keeley (Mick's) neighbour, comrade, and fellow civil servant frequently travelled with him to work in the now lawless Belfast. It was more economical for them to travel together. More economical, and safer, but also more dangerous if people learned about their different religious persuasions.

In response to the ongoing disruption of roadblocks and general traffic delays, Flexi hours were introduced in the civil service, so Mick and Ivan started working at different times. As a safety precaution when travelling alone, both friends decided to alternate cars and plan different routes to work. They frequently plotted on changing cars, travel times and routes to simply stay alive.

Government employees had become the new targets. Legitimate targets, as described by Aldo the suave Italian. The third generation he frequently announced proudly. Aldo got involved on the fringes of the local active para-militaries in the late 70s. The 'Provos'. His father was shot and killed by the Ulster Volunteer Force (UVF) for simply being Catholic. A few years later, his older brother was murdered. Executed, for reasons the family could only guess at. Aldo was hence monitored as a person of interest to the authorities. The family's home phone was tapped. During the Demetrius roundup of suspected Catholics, he was interned for eleven months, held without trial, and was finally released due to a lack of evidence of involve-ment in any illegal activities. Due to his Catholicism and family history, he was suspected of being an IRA member.

Belfast's Troubles began to escalate and Mick's civil service office, in Chichester Street, was bombed. Thank-fully a warning was issued. As he and his co-workers stood below the cordoned-off area in the city, they watched as the building was blown to smithereens. Ivan worked in a different building. The IRA bombing campaign closed Belfast down. Security gates were erected to limit access to the centre of the city. To make everyone a little safer, the civil service decided to move the staff from the bombed building and Ivan's office into other government offices at the opposite end of the city. Increased security was also provided.

Soon after the bombing, Mick's co-worker/friend was shot and killed while waiting for a bus to get to work in Belfast. Joe Mac, as they affectionately called him in the office. A big innocent catholic. A second civil servant colleague was targeted around the same time. He narrowly escaped the clutch of death as he boarded a taxi. The bullets whizzed by wide of the mark. The city of Belfast was truly a city to be feared.

Those murders, as well as others, were referred to as retaliation murders. Murders allegedly committed by the UVF and IRA. Aldo was sure that civil service employees had been deliberately targeted many years later. He was in the know by then, saying that all sides participated in those breathtakingly evil killings. He truly knew the beast of which he spoke.

Separatist groups, in addition to UVF and PROVOS, both illegal paramilitary organisations, began to form. The INLA was one of these groups and admitted to some shootings, broadcasting their murderous deeds in the local press. Catholic factions were now murdering Catholics if they fitted their mission. Similarly, protestants murdered their own, for related reasons, all in the name of 'The Cause', tit for tat murders or simply because they weren't Protestant enough. When a Catholic was shot by the opposition, a few days later a Protestant or several were shot in retaliation. Men and the occasional woman were being killed because of their religion every day.

Living in constant fear of the violence that exploded

during the conflict, the wives of the two civil servant neighbours forged a pact not to watch or listen to the news as a personal survival strategy. It was a bonus just to see their men return safely home every day. April, Ian's wife continued to drop in on Sarah and over a cuppa or four give sound feeding and sleep advice for Sarah's kids. They continued with a sense of normalcy as best they could.

Over the years, Sarah and Mick's family grew. Arthur was born in March 1980. Jude, his 9-year-old brother, shortened Arthur's name to Art. To accommodate the growing family, Mick began planning to expand the house in Knockgiven Park. Sarah was initially pleased as Mick was a perfectionist. Besides his football training and matches, everything he did was well measured, calculated and controlled. In some ways, this was a reflection of his work in the civil service, which at least brought some stability to their, often chaotic, lives.

Sarah listened to him talk through the plans almost every day, hoping he would give up his ever-increasing ideas about how it should be completed under his close supervision. Breaking out into cold sweats at the mere mention of all the proposed work, Sarah was unable to talk him out of it. Typical, organised mind she reminded herself as she tried coming up with alternative plans to his extension. Ideas were sketched on A4 sheets on the dining room table. Every week, adjustments in neat perfection and additions were made.

Their fifth child, Art, was settling into a nice routine.

Sarah was nearing the end of her maternity leave, and she would soon be returning to her nursing post, two nights a week. She sometimes felt overwhelmed juggling the school schedules of her older children and arranging childcare for the new baby. Mick's determination to make additions and renovations to their house exacerbated that anxiety.

During her precious few hours alone at the hairdressers one Saturday afternoon, Sarah read the Armagh Observer newspaper. It was folded on the homes for sale section on the waiting chair beside her. A sudden plan formed in her mind. Her plan. She remembered her brother-in-law talking about a detached house for sale near where he lived. The house was advertised in the newspaper. It was in a small cul-de-sac just a few doors from the cousins' homes, located a few fields away from where they now lived. As Sarah waited her turn at Molly's Hairdressers, she was taunted by the for-sale notice and photos of this house. She had been to the house for a party a few years back, so she knew it was spacious and that the children would have their cousins nearby to play with. Sara was confident about moving again. This four-bedroom house was close to their current home, Mick's mother's shop, and his brother's house. Leaving their neighbours and friends behind would be difficult, but they would not be so far away that their frequent encounters would cease altogether.

Cajoling her husband into bidding for the house was easier than she imagined. Mick was surprised at how quickly the new house was bought. Sarah's frequent visits from April would sadly come to an end. April would be missed.

Ivan, always willing to help, had borrowed his father's lorry to help with the move. On the morning of the move, Sarah went to the new house. Mick stayed behind to organise their already packed furnishings, but despite his meticulous planning, it was a completely chaotic day. The children were farmed out to their new neighbours and cousins, who lived only a few houses away so Sarah and Mick could unpack a little without too much trouble. As the evening drew to a close, the kids were dropped off and the excited Keeley family began to settle into their new home, glad to continue living in untroubled, quiet surroundings. However, even that would eventually change.

Talented at bricklaying, a skill Ivan had learned whilst working with his father at weekends, offered to help Mick tidy up their large unruly garden in their new Richmond Gardens home. It was going to be a mammoth task. He built a low wall with Armagh stone to section off the large, sloped garden and with Mick's dutiful help he created a beautiful rockery where a section of the garden was very rough and uneven.

The area in which Keeley's new home was located became a flight path for helicopters returning from missions. Returning to base after attending the aftermath of bombing and shooting incidents. The whirring and whining noise from those slow flights became the norm.

As the Keeleys settled into their new home, a home they had chosen to live in for the rest of their lives, their survival modes continued. Their sense of normalcy was soon shattered, however.

With all the travelling to and from work and concern for their safety, Ivan became anxious and uneasy with his frequent commutes to Belfast. Mick was taken by surprise when Ivan disclosed that he was leaving his job during one of their occasional evenings out. He worried now more than ever about his travel plans to work.

'When I was young, I always wanted to be a policeman, but you had to meet certain requirements to join the RUC. I do not have the height requirement to join,' he declared. Mick and Sarah knew there was more to come as they listened. Ivan was a practising Protestant. The couple along with their two boys went to Sunday service every week and they often met up with Sarah and Mick's family after Sunday mass. There was always some friendly slagging and banter during those get-togethers. Amid the ongoing tensions in Northern Ireland, a Police Auxiliary RUC part-time force was created to assist the police. The application forms did not ask about height. Ivan's interview and background check were successful.

Mick missed his friend's company on his journey to work. Since they no longer lived side by side, the two couples met less frequently, and when they did get together it was inevitable that the conversation would include work-related difficulties. Mick always offered advice to Ivan on his safety, knowing Ivan could not discuss his new part-time job or duty. Ivan on the odd occasion accepted Mick's advice. Mick's mantra included Ivan changing his travel routes often, especially when he went to help his father's construction business in the countryside. He needed to ensure his home was secure and his car was always locked in the garage when not in use. He gave numerous titbits of advice, such as not answering the door unless you know who it is. Advice he rarely made use of himself.

During the next five years, Ivan continued to work part-time with the police. When he was not on police duty, he helped his father with his fledgling construction company. Mick also changed jobs. He grew weary of the never-ending murderous factions and bombings in Belfast, so he applied to a new area of work with the Ministry of Agriculture. Leaving the big city office to work closer to home.

Mick and Sarah usually watched the news together in the late evening when the younger children were in bed asleep, and the helicopters were in rest mode. One evening, the Helicopters began to circle over the city like crazy. The Keeleys were watching a BBC News report on the shooting of a man in Armagh City. 'Murder Mile' was the headline story of the evening. Masked men gunned him down at his place of work in front of his two children. His girls. Sarah knew right away who it was. With her heart beating faster she informed Mick of her thoughts,

'I think it's Ivan. Targeted probably because he had served in the Auxiliary Police Force. His office is the only business in that part of the street. It must be him.'

'No way' Mick irritably responded.

The couple listened more intently as the details unfolded, and it began to sink in that Sarah was right.

'Is he another one of those targets?' Mick muttered softly as he rubbed his forehead in a state of shock.

By then, Ivan had quit his part-time job with the RUC. His focus was to work in the building trade with his father, who was planning to retire soon. Having opened a small office in town, Ivan expanded the modest family-owned company.

Jude Keeley, 14, the eldest son was at the local Cross Community Youth Club that evening. He was encouraged by Sarah to enjoy his teenage years. The club was close to where the shooting took place. As Jude walked to the youth club, he would often pass Ivan's newly opened building construction office. Knowing Ivan's girls might be there, he sometimes called in. They too enjoyed being a member of the club. Luckily, and indeed luck sometimes prevailed in those times, Jude did not call in to see his pals that evening. He arrived home, unaware of what had happened, taking the shortcut over the fields. Wondering what all the hugs and kisses from his teary-eyed parents were about, he had never felt more loved.

Early the next day, a Sunday, Sarah wanted to comfort

April at her home. To support her friend. To console and help her. Due to police presence in the area, she was unable to access April's housing estate on Saturday evening. Cups of tea were flowing as she eventually arrived at her home. Her sister, relatives and friends from the area served tea and cake to visitors.

April was grey faced with shock. Devastated. Throngs of people arrived to offer their condolences. Her friends made up the majority of the mourners. Ivan's remains arrived from the hospital later that day. Mick and other mourners, including those who had previously worked with Ivan, met the remains as they arrived in the city and followed them to April's home. The coffin remained closed when it was taken in and was laid to rest on its trellises in the family's living room. Sarah will never forget how some of the women who came to mourn treated her. People she knew well, nursing colleagues, and Protestant neighbours from The Park. When she attempted to initiate a conversation with them, they ignored her, pretended she wasn't there or shunned her. As the crowd thinned out, leaving only April's sisters and Protestant friends behind, the feeling of being part of some blame became more apparent. Sarah used to be friends with those people when she lived in The Park, so she understood why their reaction was so strong. She was Catholic. Seen as a 'side'. The side that targeted and shot Ivan. There was an overwhelming sense of sadness and shock among all of the young families in The Park.

April and Ivan's religious practices dictated that only men could walk behind the funeral procession on the way to their nearby church for the ceremony and burial. Women, wives, mothers, and relatives rode in the hearse. Mick took his place in the group, carrying the coffin of his friend out of the estate. It brought tears to Sarah's eyes as she watched through the window of April's home. Noticing the police and press presence Sarah didn't care who saw her or Mick as the cameras rolled making the news headlines of the day. He had pride of place. April hugged Sarah as she stepped out to take her seat, with her girls in the funeral car. It was a clear indication of her approval and their close friendship and helped to block out how some of her former neighbours had shunned her.

Several friends and family members visited April regularly over the following years. Whenever April and Sarah discussed Ivan's death, the sadness she felt at losing him always bubbled to the surface. Committed to death by those murderous thugs was how April described it. She never used the word Catholic. The PROVOS claimed they were responsible for his murder. Young men with warped minds who were once-catholic.

The friendship between the two families continued. Despite meeting up less often, they tried to keep in touch often. April's girls grew up fast. Tanya, the oldest, went to college in Dublin, where she eventually married a Catholic boy. They live just outside of Dublin now and April loves to visit and babysit the grandchildren. Her younger daughter lives with her long-term boyfriend closer to home.

April eventually left Knockgiven Park. 'The park'. She settled close to her sister in a picturesque village outside of the town. Sarah and Mick continue to exchange Christmas cards and gifts with April. They occasionally run into her in the supermarket near her village or in the city. They are always delighted to chat, but the memories of those horrendous times linger in all their minds. They no longer discuss those happenings directly. Sarah knows that someday soon those floodgates of memories will open, leaving their bitter legacy behind. Their grandchildren will learn from her that war is futile, and that good politics will guarantee fairness for everyone.

Smashed

As it receded from her mind and she began to sleep better, Sarah realised that on the evening of 'The Smash', she was pregnant once again.

Life was difficult during the 'Troubles' when road-blocks and random police checks became commonplace.

By the late seventies and early eighties, bombings and shootings had increased in Northern Ireland. Ordinary people who had not been directly affected and lived in safe enclaves just got up, dusted themselves down and went about their daily lives, a necessary means of survival.

Michael and Sarah lived in a relatively new housing complex on the edge of Armagh City, close to Michael's favourite Gaelic football field. Because of the 'Troubles', Mick, as he was called by his teammates, rarely got a chance to play on that field anymore.

They lived in a complex overlooking the countryside, not more than a half-mile from the almost daily turmoil of Irish Street. Their modest, modern semi-detached house was within their means, particularly now that Sarah had been granted paid maternity leave. Lizzy, another staff nurse and Sarah were the first in their hospital to avail of it.

Until the 1970s, paid maternity leave was not available. Nurses were required to leave their jobs when their babies were due before then. After the baby was born and they had found suitable childminders, they could apply for a post again. Up until then, most nurses in Northern Ireland were Catholic, as nursing was a low-paying profession. As the sixties ended, wages, conditions, and pensions improved, and nursing was becoming a respected profession. Protestant women and men also became nurses.

Soon, Protestants held most senior posts, such as ward sisters, charge nurses, matrons, and deputy matrons. As Catholic women left their positions to raise their expanding families, they rose quickly up the ranks. Catholics were forbidden to use contraceptives, so paid maternity leave was a godsend to young mothers in the nursing field.

The new maternity leave 'Act' was ignored when it came to buying houses. As pregnancy leave generally prevented women from earning a steady wage, only men's pay was considered for mortgage repayments. Therefore, when Sarah and Mick decided to move, Mick's job security and salary level, along with the favourable deposit they received from the sale of their Irish Street home, enabled them to do so.

Leaving Irish Street was a great pleasure for the family. Although their new housing estate was blissfully quiet, they still missed their caring neighbours who had experienced so many scary and dangerous incidents with them. The new neighbours were friendly and helpful. Finally, 'The Troubles' seemed far away.

Sarah, Mick, and their growing family continued to live on the edge of the city as the years passed. They were never raided or searched in their new home. None of the homes in this housing estate was. The consensus was that 'the powers that be' had a handle on who was who and their affiliations.

Nevertheless, Army searches and raids resumed in other areas. A spike in shootings occurred when new roadblocks were set up near the Gaelic field near their previous home. Now that internment had become well established, young, often innocent men who were believed to be members of illegal armed groups were rounded up and imprisoned. Families of those jailed without trial were perceived to be organizing anti-government parties with covert meetings in the homes near 'the field'. Most residents of that area on the outskirts of the city were Catholics.

When Sarah informed him that she had discovered the alarming discovery of phone tapping, Mick was shocked, so he insisted he answer the phone when he got home to hear what had happened. A series of clicks were heard when the phone rang, and the receiver was lifted. There was an intermittent buzzing, and when you spoke, an echo filled the background. Initially, those in their area assumed that it was a bad connection. As it continued others complained to the phone companies, but there was no resolution. It became known that phones were being tapped, which led to many curious and cautious conversations. Authorities later confirmed that some phones in certain areas had been tapped and recorded.

In his absence, his mother helped to take care of the children. At the far end of Armagh City, she had a little grocery store, and if Sarah had an evening outing planned with a friend, she would generously babysit for her. She had a calm and easy way of interacting with the children. Whenever she visited, she brought sweets, chocolates, and a different storybook to read to Jude and Eimear. A true gem.

One summer evening, Sarah drove her new car to fetch granny while a neighbour supervised the children. Turning the corner and passing below the Gaelic field she crossed onto the main road they rarely used, a more direct route to where the children's granny lived. Sarah was alarmed when she saw several British Army Land Rovers and Saracen's approaching at speed toward the crossroads. As she slowed down, she guessed that they were most likely on a mission to raid Greenfields Estate. The cavalcade of warlike vehicles seemed to travel in the middle of the road, leaving little room for other traffic.

At that time, the Saracens were used in the most troubled areas of Northern Ireland. One of them was Armagh. These heavy-duty six-wheeled armoured vehicles, similar to military tanks, were designed to fend off petrol bombs, bullets, and incendiary devices. Although no war had been declared in the province, they were brought in as part of the Motorman operation to regain the 'no-go areas' controlled by residents. In Sarah's opinion, these vehicles would have been more at home in South Africa where Apartheid was in force.

Sarah's neighbourhood was not yet being policed. There was a general belief among Northern Irish people that the Army was using 'The Troubles' as a training ground. By not stating it as a war it gave them the freedom to use covert heavy-handed tactics.

When the last of these monstrous vehicles approached, weaving all over the place, Sarah, the only driver approaching them, pulled in as quickly as she could at the gateway to a disused factory and stopped. Feeling that this wasn't enough, she unbuckled her seatbelt and moved over to the passenger seat just moments before the Saracen crashed into the right side of the car. The Saracen failed to stop. Her gorgeous, new blue Renault 12 was ripped open like a tin can, just missing the steering wheel. Ruined.

Pale and trembling. Sarah's heart was beating fast. After a few minutes, she sat up and swung her legs over with eyes sparking fire and nostrils wide. On the opposite side of the road, families emerged from their homes to view the noisy Army convoy, which was speeding by. No one came to help. As soon as she realised they were watching the roadblock further down the road, leading to the Villa Homes, she knew no one had dared move. Red in the face, she quickly jumped out of the car, grabbing her bag and keys as she went. As she stomped purposely back towards the roadblock, she was aware that all eyes were on her. However, no one crossed over. They were frozen at the moment. They stared from their front doors, softly chattering about her and the smashed car. She didn't care.

As a qualified staff nurse specializing in psychiatry, Sarah worked for some years at an early treatment facility. When staffing was low, she was also expected to assist in the 'General Wards' in the attached large general hospital. Being a good listener and controlling her emotions, she had treated many patients with bomb-related wounds and individuals who had been traumatized by 'The Troubles'.

Sarah approached the cordoned-off area at a fast pace and was met by a soldier pointing his rifle loosely to the ground, while others emerged with rifles from Land Rovers and Saracens.

'Stop mam,' he firmly ordered as he raised his gun. 'You cannot pass, you must leave,' he stated in a thick Scottish accent. 'What is your name?'

A young policeman quickly appeared. In softer tones, he too advised her to stop and go back down the road. When she had gathered her thoughts, standing straight with her shoulders squared, she pointed out the wreckage of her recently purchased blue car on the roadside.

'Who are these armed strangers asking me who I am,' she bellowed. 'No. I'm not going anywhere. One of your large Saracens smashed my car, but no one stopped. Is everyone so indifferent to what has happened? Is no one concerned that I may have been hurt? Do they not feel anything, or did they not know what happened?' She voiced short of screaming. 'Did you not see it?'

Sarah knew she was in unfamiliar territory as the officer repeated his firm advice to her. In the air, she detected a strong odour of alcohol. A little way ahead she saw multiple blue paint smears along one Saracen's right side, amongst the jumble of poorly parked and now empty Land Rovers and Saracens. The soldiers had abandoned their transport and hurried off on their raid mission as a surprise was the key to those intrusive missions. She repeated, raising her voice.

'I'm not leaving,' she assured the policeman, 'so you will walk me safely to my home just around the corner, through this barricade. My children are alone, and I must say that it smells strongly of alcohol here.'

She noticed the soldier standing next to them looking away sheepishly. She added, 'there's a Saracen over there covered in blue paint. That paint came from my wrecked car.'

On that late summer's evening, as the young policeman craned his neck past her, that distance now lit by the edge of the city lights, the young policeman saw the true scene. As he softened his stance and told her once again that she should leave, the stench of alcohol in the air must also have been apparent to him.

'Sorry, my hands are tied, I have to follow orders,' he nervously uttered.

Sarah was not willing to change her mind. Desperate to get home, she spoke again, a little less angrily, but with firm determination. She brushed past the armed soldier, saying, 'I'm going around you. My home is just around the corner. The one on the hill with the tall chimneys.' Pointing the direction out to the policeman, she added, 'You will come with me, and if I'm shot, it will be your fault.'

Due to the strange situation and perhaps the stress she was unwilling to give in to, she felt as though time was passing, as if in a dream. After whispering to the soldier holding the gun, he said, 'Hold on a minute.'

He walked towards a police Land Rover parked a little away, where he appeared to be talking to a person wearing a more formal, senior uniform. By this time, the evening light was dimming as loud bangs on doors usually caused by the butts from rifles echoed in the air. It seemed that the soldiers shouting orders were getting louder. Sarah became restless while standing amid the surrounding huddle of abandoned Army vehicles. She was losing patience and was growing increasingly anxious to go home. Checking her wristwatch, she realised how quickly time was passing. She felt sick of all the military actions.

While the 'Troubles' and escalating Army actions were wearing her down, she stepped purposefully forward, weaving her way through the blockade, not caring what happened as long as she reached home to her children.

Police Constable Derick Smith R.U.C. she had noted on his lapel earlier, soon reappeared at her side and offered to walk her home. As they stepped around the Army vehicles and up the hill to the corner of the crossroads, they did so swiftly without a word.

The children were asleep as she waved from the kitchen window to her neighbour and friend, signalling thanks again and everything is all right. Her friend's home was directly behind them, but on a lower level facing out on the Caledon Road, one of the main routes into the Monaghan border. Realising that he was still standing outside, she walked back down the hallway toward him.

'How can I help you, mam? Do you need a doctor? Is there anyone I can contact for you?' He asked nervously as she approached.

He is a gentle and caring soul, Sarah thought. Police attending raids was a new tactic that was introduced after rogue U.D.R soldiers went on late-night illicit rampages shooting at homes of perceived dissidents in the city. He is just someone doing his job, she reasoned. Feeling she could cope now that she was home, she politely declined the young police officer's offer of assistance. Sarah thanked him and said she understood his position as he left to return to his unit down the hill. She remembered the R.U.C. were often called in to aid nursing staff in the 'Early Treatment Unit' of the hospital when aggressive patients threatened them. Sometimes they assisted with formal admissions of seriously ill and unpredictable patients. Her thoughts softened.

Feeling a little nauseated she made excuses to her mother-in-law over the phone as to why she hadn't needed her, she ended their conversation a little abruptly, saying that the baby was crying. Rather than upset Mick, she didn't call him. We'll get used to these 'Troubles' again, she thought.

Bolting the doors Sarah climbed the stairs to the bedroom. Having assured herself again that the children were asleep, she began to shake and shiver uncontrollably. She climbed into bed and reflected on what had just happened, especially after all the mayhem in Irish Street. After finally falling asleep sobbing, she slept well but woke up with a sudden feeling of nausea. While she went to check on the two-year-old toddler whose older siblings were busy talking and preparing to be picked up for school at the far end of Armagh, she mused to herself, 'I'm sick of these times'.

They had several routes into and out of their new neighbourhood. Usually, the family travelled out to the right which took them closer to access city centre shops. The nearby estate had not yet witnessed any Army raids. Security tactics were changing. In the beginning, the Army often entered the estate through its formal entrance closer to the city. 'Raiding' as it was known from the back road out was a new operational strategy.

Mick was due home that Friday afternoon and she knew he would look after the details of the accident.

Sarah calmed down as the day progressed. The Army or the police had not made any contact. Having given the young policeman their phone number, she fully expected a response or visit after he reported the incident.

Neither a friend nor a neighbour called to offer help or soothing words. The smashed-up car outside the factory gate might not yet have been recognized by anyone who knew her. Perhaps no one wanted to be seen getting involved. During their troubled times, people were generally very cautious. With the toddler to look after and homework to manage with the other siblings, she thankfully had a busy day.

Mick's heart pounded in his chest when he arrived home in the early evening with concern for his family. He had not known about the crash. His taxi driver took him through the main road where they spotted the abandoned car sitting on the roadside. Upon seeing the extent of the damage to the car, he was quite shocked, not knowing if any of his family was hurt.

After hugs, he listened to his wife describe what happened upon his return home. Upon confirming that Sarah and their little family were unharmed, his initial sense of rage began to wane. Mick rang the police and gave the details of what happened to what sounded like a grumpy, disinterested officer. He hoped the officer would document their entire conversation. Since his father was a retired policeman, he always made allowances for some police actions.

When they told their local garage owner the details, he was somewhat shocked but assured them he would pick up the car before nightfall. He promised to get back in touch on Monday to discuss the matter and to take some photos of the car and of where the crash occurred. Additionally, the family solicitor was contacted, and the bones of the events were explained to him. He too would call back on Monday to schedule an appointment. Knowing that his phone calls were likely being monitored, Mick felt less intrusive this time. The phone tapping would be a good backup, he mused as he listened to the continuous clicks, buzzing, and echoes.

During that Monday's conversation in the solicitor's office, the solicitor's looked into Sarah's eyes as he went over the details of that evening.

'Do you have any injuries, do you sleep well, do you have flashbacks, are you pregnant?' He added apologetically.

'None of them' Sarah stammered.

She was not interested in invasive or clarifying appointments with medical professionals. She just wanted compensation for the wrecked car sorted so they could purchase a replacement and move on with their lives. Moving on was one of her strong suits.

Mr. Hughes was known for his professionalism as a solicitor. A straightforward, honest speaker. He warned them that any legal details involving the Army would be laborious and slow. In these matters he advised them, they were noted for denial.

'Beware', he added, 'you may get an Army counterclaim. I have dealt with their solicitors in the past, but even if it takes months, perhaps even a year or so, I intend to win. Hire a car through your garage in the meantime and I will ensure payment for the hire will be included in the writ.' He glanced at Sarah once more.

'If you have any injuries, no matter how small, let me know.'

After some time had passed and their lives returned to a semblance of normality within the constraints of those times, the family decided to move again. The children's school was near their grandmother's shop at the other end of the city. Their uncle was the deputy principal, and it was reputed to be one of the best primary schools in the area. Currently, Sarah had to push the baby's pram over a mile to pick up the kids from school in the evenings. The kids used to receive a free early morning ride to school from a kindly neighbour, but that ended when his son moved on to secondary school. As Sarah's family grew, her hours of night duty were reduced; two weekly nights were welcome.

Mick's colleague, with whom he commuted to work, mentioned there was a house for sale near him. Their carpool agreement was economical and safe in numbers on their journeys. Sarah and Mick decided it was time to move to a better neighbourhood.

The opportunity to buy a new house in a mixed-religion area was a blessing. The main reason they chose to move to this new area was the proximity of the primary school, their grandmother's shop, and their home. It was also uplifting that it was in a neutral and hostile-free area. There had never been any military raids or bomb scares in the area. The area was deemed not to be a threat. It was a new housing complex built within a predominantly Protestant area that was slowly becoming mixed. Their house in Villa Homes sold quickly for a nice profit.

1976 was the year they moved to Knockgiven Park. The month was April, six months after their car was damaged by the Army. Hughes, the family's solicitor, kept them informed about the continuing barrage of legal correspondence between him and the Army. It was during this time that 'The Troubles' sadly intensified.

Life went on for Mick and Sarah's family and settling into their new home hassle-free was like stepping into a whole new world. The children walked safely to school and played outside all day. A large patio window in their lovely 1970s home allowed Sarah to observe them with ease.

Answering a loud and insistent knocking at the front door, Sarah assumed it must be a parcel arriving from the post office. She opened the door and was shocked to see two soldiers standing 'To Attention' on her doorstep. She began to think something bad had happened to Mick or a close family member. She quickly gave way to their abrasive words as they thrust a large brown envelope into her hands.

'This Mam is a special delivery of a writ from headquarters, and we need your signature to confirm delivery.'

Despite being just over six months pregnant and feeling tired, but mostly relaxed, nothing seemed to faze Sarah, not even the delivery of legal documents. When her car was smashed all those months ago, she knew their garage owner had the photos. She was confident with their solicitor's ability to ensure their rights would be upheld. Her pregnancy was proceeding as normal and she was sure the baby was unharmed.

Once the children were in bed, the couple opened the documents and were shocked to discover they related to a counterclaim from the Army. For them, waiting all this time to deliver those papers was a mystery. The legal jargon and notations made for heavy reading and most of them read beyond their scope of understanding.

Mr. Hughes, however, was not surprised. While discussing the claim, he noted Sarah's advanced pregnancy. He wished the couple well, adding that it was too late to seek any other compensation. Despite the counterclaim, he remained confident that their claim would be successful. Sarah was not concerned on her behalf. The only thing she wanted was for their deserved claim to be upheld and the proceedings to be over. After several months, a modest settlement was reached that just about covered the legal costs and replacement of the car. After their ordeal, Mick and Sarah were able to get back to normal life and looked forward to the imminent birth of their new baby.

Several years later, in the late 1970s, Mick was called to a meeting at the Army Barracks with some top-ranking Army officers. Senior civil servants from his office also attended. Mick was assigned to take notes. After the meeting, a chatty officer sat down for a cup of tea with Mick. They touched on their experiences and the car crash as they spoke about their jobs and The Troubles. The officer disclosed that he was very familiar with that incident. He related the story of the night it happened. A regiment of the Army was on their last night of duty in Armagh City. Some of the soldiers were drinking in 'The Soldiers Mess' when the call came in to execute the raid. A heavy drinker had driven the Saracen that smashed the car. All of this conversation was 'off the record.' That particular soldier had since been discharged from his regiment; the officer told Mick.

On hearing this Sarah realised that she was vindicated and was in no way to blame for the smash. It was not a figment of her imagination when she mentioned possible drinking before the raid and the smell of alcohol in the air as well. No injuries were a good result. The baby was born safely. But Sarah's memory of that evening is ingrained in her. In her later years, Sarah recounts all of those happenings over a glass of wine to anyone who will listen. With a bit of drama and a little humour thrown in. Above all, she is grateful that her little immediate family remained intact and trouble-free.

There is No Flag Worth Dying For

The Bullet

Bombings and shootings had become more targeted, and warnings usually pre-empted them. However, there was concern that recruitment drives in local communities, by now younger war-faring factions, would create a new concern for parents. There were pockets of splinter groups within the IRA. Despite the implementation of The Good Friday Agreement, none of the younger factions of those groups intended to cease their activities. They had other motives that weren't necessarily for the love of their Country.

Sarah was out of breath as she rushed to answer the phone that was ringing loudly and persistently.

'Please can you come quickly to our house? I need you. Something has happened.'

'Yes of course,' her mother stammered.

As Louise opened her front door to take in the milk that Monday morning, she noticed an unusual-looking copper piece sitting beside the bottles. After picking it up, she screamed and dropped it. It was a bullet.

Eddie, her husband was introduced to the Keeley family

and home for the first time two years before. Sarah admired his bravery when he arrived that afternoon, knowing that Louise's father, Mick, did not approve of him. He was not pleased to hear that his favourite daughter was getting married so young. After a grumpy hello and reluctance handshake, Mick fled to the pub, whispering to Sarah in cross tones, to find out more about him.

Sarah also had a poor misguided impression of Eddie when she first met him on Louise's birthday. He seemed loud and boastful. She hoped that the romance wouldn't last. She now knew he was a nice young man. It was obvious that he cared deeply for her daughter. As he talked about his job, within his family's double-glazing company, his chatty manner put her at ease. During his visit, Louise's siblings asked lots of questions, dispelling any sense of awkwardness in the room. Seeing Louise's laughter and smile gave Sarah confidence that things would be okay. Reluctant to probe too deeply, Sarah left the young couple to spend some time alone in their 'Good Room'. A sitting room that was rarely used as her family tended to congregate in the living room where the television had pride of place.

Eddie's sister Margo was moving to England with her family. Many young families fled the mayhem during the Troubles. Margo offered Eddie and Louise their relatively new home, so the young couple were delighted to move in and pay her modest rent. Thus, their desire to marry as soon as possible.

Louise's parents encouraged their children to go out and enjoy their young lives. The worst of those times in Northern Ireland had passed by the time their older children reached their teenage years. When stopped and questioned by Soldiers, they advised them to remain calm and to avoid bomb scare areas. To help calm Mick and Sarah's underlying worries, they encouraged them to be honest about where they were going when they were heading out.

Sarah drove the short distance to the countryside in a hurry, her mind in turmoil, to find Louise in tears, shaking uncontrollably. She embraced her, trying to ease her anxiety. She was ashen, her skin appeared blue around her edges, and she felt cold. Baby Annie slept peacefully in her pram.

'I found a bullet on our front porch, this morning. It looked like it had been placed there deliberately among the milk bottles. Eddie said it hasn't been fired,' she exclaimed, gasping for breath.

Eddie had gone to work after receiving assurances from Louise that she was okay. Agreeing, with him, there had to be a reasonable explanation for the bullet. But those vanished as her panic set in when she found herself alone with their newborn. Her immediate concern was getting someone to share her panic with, advise her and keep them safe. The little one was still fast asleep.

'This is awful,' she sobbed. 'What did we do wrong to deserve this?'

Sarah's mind was awash with all sorts of unfounded reasoning. It must be some kind of warning. Or a pre-emptive notice of intention to demand protection money from the family's double-glazing firm. A small company that thrived and was in huge demand due to the destructive bombs that had exploded all over Northern Ireland. Glaziers were being made rich by the Troubles, so the IRA thought it was only fair that they also get their fair share. The provisional IRA, the PROVOS, especially around Belfast were extorting protection money and threatening and disrupting workers by destroying their premises and materials. The building industry was predominantly Catholic and therefore controlled by the IRA. The ill-gotten funds were used to finance their war campaign to achieve a united Ireland by force of arms. The conflict had been declared over. Other explanations sprang to mind.

'Could it be a stray farmer's bullet?' Sarah offered, 'from a neighbouring farm?'

'No mum,' Louise replied. 'Eddie says it hasn't been fired and was placed on our doorstep with intent. Some kind of dark message, I think.'

Louise tried to stifle her sobs as she began to express her suspicions about the probable, maybe sinister motives.

The nearby Breamount village was alert to all the local activity in their tight-knit community. The farmers looked out for each other, returning stray cows, sheep, and dogs to their owners. Exchanging information about the latest beef prices and all kinds of agriculture gossip. Rarely missing unusual activities of people and news updates. Eddie's dad had already advised them to not contact the police, Louise explained.

'Not yet anyway. Let's think about it first.' He added. New brightly coloured police cars were often spotted out on their country road. They were in close contact with a young local man, a suspected tout.

'I'll ask Tommy to make a few enquiries,' Eddie's father continued. 'He knows all the goings-on around here.' Tommy was a local middle-aged farmer who worked part-time as a glazier for their company. Maintaining his farm by eking out a living. He had a brother who was a local police officer. Something he kept quiet about. Very few people knew as he had been living in England for several years.

Young men from the area had set up a branch of the INLA in the village. A breakaway group that disagreed with the PROVOS softening attitudes. They held secret meetings in a disused crumbling factory that had not gone unnoticed by neighbours. The comings and goings were much discussed among the elderly. Louise turned her attention to other reasons for placing the bullet on their doorstep. On the living room couch, she sat down beside Sarah with a cup of tea and discussed what was on her mind.

Growing up in Knockgiven Park, a Cul-de-sac estate in Armagh, Louise was fortunate to have several friends her age living nearby. They began to drift apart as they approached their teenage years. One of those friends' older brothers Kevin bought a home near them. We all wondered how he could afford that house.

A few days later Louise & Eddie received a hand-delivered note pushed through their letterbox. Under the cover of darkness, most likely. Eddie was ordered to come to Braemount to meet with 'The Boys'. A covert name for those young local INLA members. After listening to good advice from his father, Eddie decided not to adhere to the command. Paddy informed him that Tommy was handling the issue, but he didn't explain how, leaving his son forever wondering how that could be possible.

After several weeks, Louise began to feel safe again and her youthful, happy form returned. Eddie's father assured her that the matter was settled.

'Put to rest' were the words he used.

This was his way of helping the young couple move on.

Sarah began to visit their house more frequently. When Eddie was at work, she helped with babysitting and kept Louise company. A semblance of normality returned to life even though the undercurrents and unrest sporadically bubbled through. Most of all, she enjoyed taking Annie for long walks in the countryside.

Baby Annie was fast asleep on a particularly sunny day as they were out walking. Approaching the crossroads on one of the country lanes she noticed a parked Police vehicle. Despite her unease, she walked towards it. As she drew closer, she noticed some quick movement and shuffling. Observing a young man, who had been chatting in the car, scramble into the back seat. She recognised him.

The young man, Kevin was an old friend's son who lived with his young girlfriend and baby in the city, close to Sarah's house. She often wondered how they could afford such a large luxurious home and the MG sports car at such a young age. It was often the subject of local gossip as Kevin didn't seem to have a steady job; he was home a lot and spent occasional mysterious overnights away alone. As Sarah passed the police car, she noticed the two officers without police caps talking to Kevin in the back seat. Her heart pounded. Pretending to look across the fields as she passed by, she walked past as casually as she could muster, turning right near the merging roads. Was it him? Is it Kevin who placed the bullet at Louise's door?

Arriving back at baby Annie's home she met Paddy in his Jeep. Coming down the lane to his son's home. Closing the door, on getting out, he moved quickly to the pram hoping for a smile and chat with his granddaughter. She was fast asleep. Paddy and Sarah settled down to a cup of tea, leaving the baby outside the patio door. As Paddy chatted away Sarah's recounted what she had encountered at the crossroads.

'I saw Kevin Mc Shane up the road, Paddy. He lives near us now and owns that large, lovely house too.'
Immediately, Paddy became flustered and began to stutter, as he often did when he was angry.

'That young whippersnapper, no good will come to that lad. He'll come to a bad end.' Sarah knew what he meant or might mean. She didn't divulge the details of how she saw Kevin.

Sarah loved the journey to County Louth to the family-owned cottage near Greenore. Driving through Newry, County Down, along the Newry Canal, through Omeath and out past Carlingford. One sunny Sunday, she was held up by a Police road check, behind a long line of cars, at the Newry canal. Near a low flattened grassy area, she saw a twisted and broken hedge. Car tracks were gorged in the earth. A red MG Sports car was pulled from the canal the day before, just where the water flowed into the sea, right on the edge of Northern Ireland and County Louth. Later in the cottage, Sarah learned that a body had been found in the vehicle. The police were checking everyone passing through the area, asking if they heard, or knew anything about what may have happened the Saturday evening before.

As time passed, these things were forgotten. Put on the back burner, as the saying goes. Eddie and Louise were reluctant to discuss the bullet again. Sarah also put it to the back of her mind. Only occasionally, did she consider the matter?

Almost a year after Kevin's death, an inquest concluded that he had been murdered. A detailed account of the findings was published in the Newry Reporter. His reasons for being in that area on that fateful Saturday were revealed. It was a mystery to his relatives why he had to report to the Garda Siochana just across the border on a fortnightly basis. Perhaps he was caught smuggling guns or engaging in some other subversive activity. At that time, the Northern Irish police were successfully cooperating with the Garda to stem illegal cross-border business. Kevin's brakes had been tampered with. The brake fluid slowly leaked from a hole punched in its housing. This was believed to have occurred in Armagh close to his home. Most likely, under the cover of darkness.

The farmers 'gossip machine' in the country near Louise's home was rolling. No doubt that he was a tout, they agreed he got his comeuppance. The young man's untimely death brought sadness as well. It was suspected that he was dispatched by his own kind. Most believed that his comrades had carried out the deed, leaving behind his young girlfriend and baby. As for Louise and Eddie, they have never forgotten the bullet left on their doorstep though the incident is rarely talked about.

Sarah, now in her later years, mulls through the fog of unforgiving memories. The useless loss of life. Mourning her friends. Often wondering how her family got through those long years of war unscathed but as Anatole Broyard author of 'Kafka Was The Rage' said "A war is like an illness, and when it's over you think you've never felt so well."

There is No Flag Worth Dying For

Falcarragh Feis

It was another hectic day at the Feis. Irish dancers milled about waiting to participate in endless competitions. Heavy hornpipe shoes drummed in the side rooms while jigs and reels were practised in every corridor of the large dance hall. The dancers' mild anxiety and hopes to win a few medals for their school were evident as repetitive dance music played on fiddles beside the three stages. Sarah's light-hearted conversations with fellow mothers and the background ambience took an emotional toll on her.

Donegal's Falcarragh village, a few miles from the dancing venue was a picturesque, tranquil getaway. Upon returning to the hotel, the dancers and their moms declared they would relax, talk about the day's competition, and have a little fun. The mothers would also have some downtime afterwards, which always included a drink or two. A little bevvy.

Vodka was the tipple of choice. In addition to the vodka, the ladies also pulled out plastic cups and lemons from their handbags. Sarah was not good at keeping up with the copious amounts the other mothers could handle. After a generous drink prepared by her friend Moira, she would feel woozy. Her small frame wasn't accustomed to handling drinks without eating first. This time she vowed inwardly not to have a second one. Assured her daughter Louise would be fine, she made excuses to have a look around the hotel and slipped away.

It was raining outside as she entered the main foyer. The hotel bar was busy. There were also some parents and children from Southern Ireland staying at the hotel. After dipping in and out of the restaurant, events hall and the hotel shop she wandered into the resident's lounge. Other than a few elderly people who spent a holiday week or more there, the space was relatively quiet. Sarah settled into a comfortable chair near the window to enjoy the view of the extensive gardens outside and the mountains beyond. This beautiful part of Ireland felt very safe and serene, far away from the troubled north.

As the rain poured from the heavens, the residents watched a loud but engaging program on a TV in the corner. Close to where she was sitting, a pleasant elderly gentleman moved a little closer and pointing at the TV whispered,

'I'm sure you're glad about this.'
Referring to the content of the broadcast.

'I hope this time it really works for all of this island. We saw your troupe of dancers arriving yesterday. Saw your cars with northern registrations. I enjoyed hearing the children's northern Irish accents when you all booked in.'

As Sarah focused, she realised the significance of this historical moment. This time, there was a real plan of commitment towards peace in Northern Ireland between all political parties and war-faring gangs. The Good Friday Agreement was unfolding, four years after the PROVOS introduced the IRA ceasefire. This was the 10th of April 1998. Sarah was captivated by the high-ranking politicians seated around a large oval table and the group of news broadcasters setting up their cameras and microphones.

The hotel's sitting room began to fill up. Guests stood around with drinks in hand watching the TV in silence. The South of Ireland was also tired of the loss of life, especially when it spilt over from the north, killing and injuring their fellow countrymen, and bringing cities and towns to their knees.

If anyone asked Sarah where she was on that historic day, she would always remember she was at a Feis in the peaceful village of Falcarragh in Donegal. The day of 'The Good Friday Agreement'. As the broadcast continued, Sarah lost track of time. Moira later appeared beside her and whispered that the others and the children were wondering where she was. Sarah left the room with tears in her eyes as the broadcast came to an end. Tears of relief and joy. Everyone else cheered and clapped.

The children's rooms grew quiet after an active evening of dance practice. They finally went to bed. Several mothers lingered in one of the bedrooms, enjoying generous refills of vodka. After Sarah re-joined the mothers and informed them of the talks, she realised no one else was interested in the broadcast. Was it because these formal dialogues have been tried before and failed, or was it the general feeling that their lives may never return to normal? Maybe it was the vodka? Comments like

'We were at this place before,'

'I don't believe it' and

'Life just goes on anyway'

dominated their relaxed, tipsy conversation before bed.

A little wound up, Sarah closed her eyes in the bunk bed below her daughter Louise's snores. While she felt a little let down by her friend's remarks, she knew some of what they said was true. During those long years, amidst all the violence, life did go on as normal, especially when bombings usually preceded by warnings, became more targeted. Families went out for meals, shows, holidays and to the pub. Unless a major incident happened and roadblocks were erected, weddings, parties and concerts etc. went on as usual. The 'stop and search' decreased over time when crossing the border. Life did go on.

The loss of life for unfortunate families and friends was always recognised and mourned. Parents were always grateful for children who were not involved and continued to study and pass their exams. People who lived outside the troubled areas were generally sheltered from the continuous Troubles.

She slept restlessly that night and dreamed of those

early years. helicopters with whirring blades crossing at high speed, sirens, bombs, gunfire echoes, coffins passing by, black smoke billowing from the bus station a few hundred yards behind their garden as they prepared a barbecue. She also dreamed of before those times. When she never heard them flying, bombing or shooting. The debris from those times enveloped her as if they were on fire, and she awoke.

Returning home from the weekend Feis, the now sober group felt a real sense of light-heartedness as the reality of the previous evening's political announcements sunk in. The children proudly displaying their hard-won medals and cups contributed to the light mood. When he picked up his wife and Louise, Mick was eager to discuss The Good Friday Agreement, saying: 'We'll vote for it, Sarah, and make our voices heard.'

Sarah would later recount her family's experiences during those long thirty years. She was able to share how her husband and children survived. How they were among the lucky ones. When Sarah's eldest son Jude was approached by recruits for the PROVOS in Derry, he decided not to join up, and she was glad she had advised him strongly against it. She recalled the last words she told Jude when he asked for advice. The conversation she never told anyone, not even, then, to his father Mick. A saying her mother often repeated,

'There is no flag worth dying for.'

There is No Flag Worth Dying For

ACKNOWLEDGEMENTS

Writing a book is harder than I thought and more rewarding than I could have ever imagined. None of this would have been possible without my great friend, Siobhan Hughes.

Thank you, Siobhan, my first editor who insisted on reading on learning I had written these stories. From reading early drafts to giving me lots of helpful advice, she was as important to this book getting done as I was. She generously spent time and patience editing and rectifying my many grammar errors and reclining their flow. Her endless encouragement, support, and belief in taking this book to a place for publishing. Thanks also to my daughter Aisling for her editorial help, keen insight, and ongoing support in bringing my stories to life. Because of their efforts and encouragement, I have a legacy to pass on to my family where one didn't exist before. I'm forever indebted.

The cover design is an adaptation of two stunning pictures from two incredible photographers on Unsplash. Thank you, Annie Spratt @anniespratt for your "Down roads we go" imagery of the two little kids. Thank you, Vince GX for the "Alive shadows" imagery of the graveyard.

And finally, thanks to my ever-patient family for their quiet tolerance throughout this process.

Printed in Great Britain
by Amazon

18216903R00102